GREAT HOUSES OF TEXAS

GREAT HOUSES OF TEXAS

LISA GERMANY | PHOTOGRAPHY BY GRANT MUDFORD

ABRAMS, NEW YORK

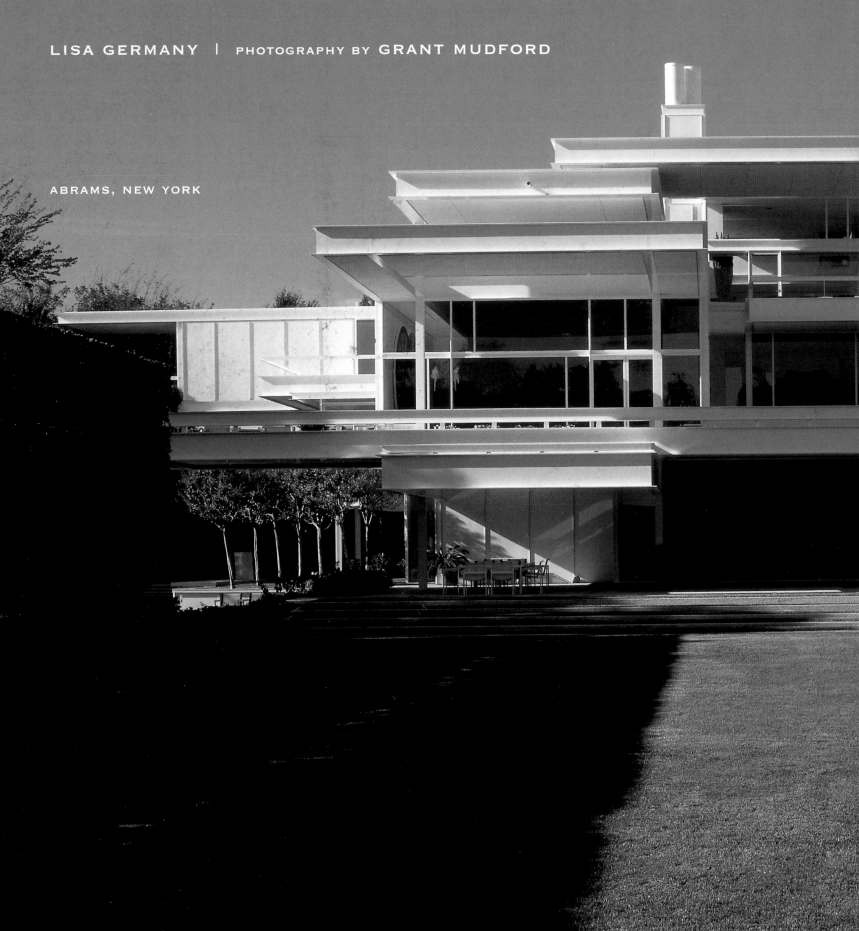

FOR MEL, WHO SHOWED ME MY HOMELAND THROUGH THE LENS OF AN ARTIST,

AND FOR ATTICUS AND PHINEAS, WHO WERE BORN UNDER THE TEXAS STAR. —LG

CONTENTS

INTRODUCTION

TEXAS, OUR TEXAS! ALL HAIL THE MIGHTY STATE!
TEXAS, OUR TEXAS! SO WONDERFUL SO GREAT!
LARGEST AND GRANDEST, WITHSTANDING EV'RY TEST
O, EMPIRE WIDE AND GLORIOUS, YOU STAND SUPREMELY BLEST.
GOD BLESS YOU, TEXAS! AND KEEP YOU BRAVE AND STRONG,
THAT YOU MAY GROW IN POWER AND WORTH THROUGHOUT THE AGES LONG.

—STATE SONG OF TEXAS, 1929

So sang schoolchildren every morning in a small West Texas town during the early days of the 1960s. Next to the staid, somewhat impenetrable words of "America"—"My country 'tis of thee . . ."—the Texas song seemed downright thrilling. Even a first grader, which I was back then, could feel a welling up of pride while belting out that string of adjectives and superlatives. Then one day, word came that Alaska really was, after all, the largest state (had been for two years), and someone had changed the words of the song to reflect the truth. But the replacement word *boldest* seemed vague, lifeless, ordinary. And so began the dim, gnawing fear that something important had been lost, some chipping away at a child's idea of Texas's hegemony.

As it turned out, nothing of the kind occurred. Texas's sense of itself hardly faltered. Its great, wide-open spaces where "the skies are not cloudy all day" were not diminished. The legends and lore embracing cowboys and cattle drives, oil and wildcatters, cotton fields and fortunes flourished as they passed from one generation to another. To have been born a Texan was to know that you were an heir to all that. And should you ever forget it, you need only travel beyond Texas's borders (even to remote corners of the earth) to be

reminded of it again: "Texas! You're from Texas?" The shock of recognition was invariably warm and welcoming, giving you the sense that who or what you were (or might turn out to be), there was the consolation that in the eyes of the rest of the world you were, at least, a Texan.

It is ironic that a land so diverse in its topography (a post–Civil War governor attempted to split it into three states) and so dogged in its code of individual rights and prerogatives could have found itself so happily united. The flag bearing a single star, held aloft as early as 1836 over the massacred soldiers at Goliad (which, along with the Alamo, provided the passion necessary to win independence), proved to be the perfect emblem for the state, symbolizing in its solitary way a clear autonomy even when the Republic was annexed by the United States in 1845. And this Lone Star, like the "lone prairie," became a slogan that was not so much about being alone or lonely, but rather about the condition of being a loner in the romantic sense, someone with an individualistic attitude. Handed down through the years, this character trait set the tone for a Texas way of life— often fiercely private, inscrutably original, and famously picturesque. However brightly America's constellation

PAGE 1: The Lasater house in Fort Worth.

PAGES 2–3: The Bass house in Fort Worth.

PAGE 4: One of the huge live oaks in the garden of the Armstrong-Ferguson house.

BELOW: The Hohenberger farmstead (1871), south of Fredericksburg. This stone house of a family who immigrated from Bremen, Germany, possesses the characteristics that continue to influence Texas architects today, including walls made of indigenous limestone and deep eaves for shelter from the sun. Photo courtesy of Carol Zimmermann, Comfort, Texas.

would shine, the Texas star would remain distinctly personal and identifiable.

Which is why a book that attempts to wrap words around Texas residential architecture requires, well, the boldest kind of critical conceit, for there is no easy codification of a Texas aesthetic; to attempt it would constitute a colossal missing of the point. Each house depicted in the following pages has its own distinctive style. There is only one overarching influence that captures even the most unwieldy of houses in its embrace, and that is the formidable Texas landscape itself. To greater or lesser extents, the landscape is always the protagonist.

Among the twenty-five homes singled out here as great examples of Texas architecture, five, which display the imprint of contemporaneous styles elsewhere, begin the story. The earliest—Woodlawn—was built in the Greek Revival style, which was at the height of fashion in 1854, just after annexation—in fact, the architect/builder, Abner Cook, borrowed details from a book entitled *The Beauties of Modern Architecture*. With its elegance and graceful situation, it masked the still very raw frontier aspect of Texas at the time. (Texas Rangers were battling Apaches as late as 1881.) By dominating the landscape, it sought to demonstrate in bold strokes that Texas was a place of culture. Similarly, the Italianate House of the Seasons in Jefferson (1872) mitigated and controlled one's sense of the landscape by means of the colored glass in its lantern, which dramatized and enhanced seasonal changes and harnessed the capricious play of the strong natural light in Texas. The frontier, through such a lens, was distant and benign; the gentility of the Deep South had found a port of entry here.

Some three decades later and eight hundred miles west, one sees how the landscape reasserts itself in the El Paso home of architect Henry Trost. Fresh from the Chicago of

Louis Sullivan and Frank Lloyd Wright, Trost would build a Prairie Style house the likes of which one would never encounter in Oak Park, Illinois. Unlike its predecessors, it did not hunker down and blend in with the flat horizon of the prairie; it rose up and complemented the mountainous terrain of the desert city. It was Prairie Style adjusted for Texas, just as Nicholas Clayton's League house was Victorian adjusted (by means of Colonial Revival details) for the sea breezes of Galveston. And in San Antonio, Atlee Ayres looked around at the subtropical, sybaritic landscape, with its imprint of Hispanic imperialism, and created a Spanish Revival style that was also unique and very particular to Texas.

But as Texas aged and the notion of place began to take on the trappings of the built environment—to the extent that a great French-style villa seemed perfectly at home among the mansions of Dallas—a passionate, unsentimental interest emerged in the humble structures of the Texas frontier. The Texas landscape for early pioneers had been the defining factor: Dwellings were shaped by the materials at hand, the need for ventilation and shelter from the fierce sun, the individual skills of the builder, and the need for protection from the ravages of less-than-welcoming natives.

Architect David Williams, who had himself grown up in a dugout on the plains of North Texas, was the first to appreciate the lessons of the pioneers and to believe that a particular Texas style could be shaped according to their tenets. With his protégé and friend, O'Neil Ford, he traveled the state photographing the frontier structure and attempted to popularize it in essays for *The Southwestern Review*. His Drane-Cook house, as grand as it is, bears the fundamental lessons he learned, and Ford's Bromberg house clearly refers to pioneer concerns, particularly the need for ventilation, which persisted until the air conditioner became commonplace in the second half of the twentieth century.

However, it was ultimately Ford, not Williams, who demonstrated how the frontier could be a point of reference for modern architecture. The values Ford espoused, both in words and in buildings, profoundly affected Texas architects and clients who found that natural forms and materials responding to the landscape emphasized the beauty of their chosen home site.

He did not teach an adherence to a particular creed or image, but under his influence some modern architects retraced the steps of pioneer builders, distilling ideas that remain potent for life in Texas even today. When Frank Welch tells how Ford taught him about the integrity of materials, or Ted Flato of Lake/Flato says Ford taught him "how things went together," they are speaking in code about the brilliance of Ford's vision for Texas architecture. One can see the relevance of frontier architecture at work in Max Levy's elegant house on a pond that has not one but two dogtrots (the old term for breezeways, which were commonly built in frontier houses). And the warm plaster of Natalye Appel's contemporary house in Cat Spring was derived from her study of the material covering the limestone and timber construction of German *fachwerk* houses in the Texas Hill Country.

Texans love the land—love to own it, use it, look at it—and while Williams and Ford may have reopened values that make the enjoyment of it not only practical but poetic, the houses gathered together here under the heading "Great Houses" have this affection in common. In the frontier way, they are stridently private, but when you find them behind brick walls, giant live oaks, or at the culmination of long, winding drives (as this book invites you to do), you can see the threads that bind them. Whether large or small, lavish or modest, urban or rural, together they unlock a vision of Texas.

Lisa Germany

1

THE IMPRINT
OF FASHION

View into the library of the Woodlawn house.

WOODLAWN

"To give you an account of his life would be, in a certain sense, to write the history of this city." So spoke the reverend Kelley Smoot at the funeral service of Abner Cook on February 24, 1884. It was true—Cook's life had spanned the entire history of Austin up to that point. He had arrived in 1839, just after Edwin Waller, who had been appointed by the Republic's president, Mirabeau B. Lamar, to build a capital city in the frontier, and he had stayed there, helping build the city from the ground up. He made his own bricks down by Shoal Creek (in the center of the city now), he owned a sawmill in the pines of nearby Bastrop to provide wood for Austin, and he worked, mostly as a carpenter, a contractor, and often as a subcontractor. And yet, though Cook's modest soul was too often lost in the bricks and mortar or millwork of someone else's structure, this "master builder" was also a designer. In a two-year period, roughly 1854 to 1856, he designed a handful of Greek Revival mansions so lovely and so beautifully proportioned as to rival the houses in that style anywhere else in the country. In the fledgling capital (where a random buffalo could still be seen wandering down Congress Avenue), these homes said that Austin had arrived. They were also a sign that the frontier was fading.

Of the five mansions that survive, including the Governor's Mansion, one—the Pease mansion, called Woodlawn—stands out as the most exemplary. It was named for E. M. Pease, the former governor of Texas, whose family occupied it for close to a hundred years before selling it to another former Texas governor, Allan Shivers. Following its long life and occasional vicissitudes, its current renovation makes it possible to gain a renewed appreciation of Cook's mastery of scale and proportion. Unlike the countless imitation Greek Revival houses across the country, the Pease mansion is a masterpiece not simply because Cook was skillful with the clichés of the Greek Revival—the columns, the capitals, the window treatments, the balconies—but because he understood that its grace depended on a certain quiet and pristine classicism.

The original client was not E. M. Pease, however, but a man named James B. Shaw, who had been comptroller for the Republic of Texas and later for the state, earning a salary that was second only to the governor's. He was a cultivated Irishman, educated at the University of Dublin, who had parlayed his salary into a fortune from real estate dealings in Texas. At the time he contacted Abner Cook,

ALTHOUGH SCHOLARS HAVE LONG BEEN AWARE THAT THE GREEK REVIVAL BEGAN IN EUROPE AND THAT IN AMERICA IT STARTED IN PHILADELPHIA AND SPREAD NORTH, SOUTH, AND WEST, IN THE PUBLIC MIND THE GREEK REVIVAL IS INDELIBLY ASSOCIATED WITH THE ANTEBELLUM SOUTH. . . .

—KENNETH HAFERTEPE, FROM *Abner Cook: Master Builder of the Texas Frontier*

PREVIOUS SPREAD: The portico of Abner Cook's fine Greek Revival house is uninterrupted by a roofline or pediment. The second floor X-and-stick balustrade around the balcony is an example of his taste for fine millwork and became a signature of his work.

OPPOSITE: View of the eastern facade, with a profile of the southern facade.

he had become engaged to a woman in New Orleans and wanted to build a house for her. But, as it turned out, she married another man, whereupon Shaw rebounded and married a different woman and had a child. But tragically, at the age of two, the child died, and soon afterward the young mother. Broken-hearted, Shaw left Austin, vowing never to return. He signed the closing documents with Pease, in fact, in Galveston.

But back when the promise of a happy domestic life still loomed, Shaw had purchased 650 acres in the hilly, wooded landscape northwest of Austin. Perhaps he knew of Cook's work from a small Federalist-style house he had built for a prominent fellow Irishman, William Ward, or from the Greek Revival house being designed simultaneously for his colleague James Raymond. In any case, Cook was on the job in early 1854, designing the house in the style he had probably first seen in the Presbyterian Church of Salisbury, North Carolina, near his birthplace. And he brought with him, apparently, his trusty copy of Minard Lafever's book *The Beauties of Modern Architecture*, in which the New York architect illustrated Greek Revival details.

The house was sited on the eastern edge of Shaw's property, facing east, and although Pease family members later subdivided their large parcel of land, they wisely kept a generous portion of it for the grounds of the house. Because the house sits deeply back from the street on a lot that is almost a full city block, it is possible to appreciate the monolithic demeanor of its front facade—a portico of six Greek columns with Ionic capitals. The southern facade, which would have also welcomed visitors from Austin, boasts three columns with Doric capitals. On each face, balconies with

Cook's characteristic X-and-stick balustrade (a remnant of the Federalist style) are extended above the central doorways. And Cook took Greek Revival details inside in the form of shouldered architraves, a variation on a pattern in Lafever's style book in which battered side moldings (which grow progressively narrower as they climb) are surmounted by wide, slightly overhanging lintels.

Cook's Grecian piers were doubtless pines from the forests around Bastrop, where he had operated his sawmill (such seems to have been the case in the Governor's Mansion, which followed closely upon the completion of this house). It is also believed that the bricks of this house—the exterior walls are three feet thick and the interior walls are two feet thick—were derived from Cook's own kilns.

The original plan was an L-shape, with a double parlor and a dining room to the left of a wide entrance corridor, and another room (a library) to the right. The central corridor was in itself a generous room, which would have run the course of the house, front to back. Its focus is Cook's Greek Revival staircase, as direct and yet graceful as the house itself. Upstairs was an exact duplicate floor plan of the downstairs, allowing for four bedrooms. The completed house had cost Shaw more than $20,000, a considerable sum in 1854.

In the middle years of the 1850s, Cook's star shined brightly, but for reasons not entirely clear, he returned to his work as a contractor and subcontractor thereafter. Nevertheless, with Woodlawn and the other remaining houses he designed, he had accomplished what the young state desperately needed—symbols of culture and refinement.

LEFT: The stairway at the entrance of Woodlawn was originally confined by a wall that enclosed the study to the right, but a previous owner removed part of that wall, opening up the space and making way for the balustrade on the right.

BELOW: After the removal of an unfortunate addition to the south portico, the dining room windows now offer a clear view of the lawn.

BOTTOM: The large living room was originally built as a double parlor until former Governor Allan and Mrs. Shivers removed the dividing wall in the late 1950s. They also repainted the house a very pale pink, replacing the dark red that had covered it during the ownership of, coincidentally, yet another former governor, E. M. Pease.

18

BELOW: Child's room with tiles of knights in purple-and-ocher armor surrounding the fireplace.

BOTTOM: Like the double parlor on the first floor, which became one long living space, the wall that divided this single space into two separate bedrooms was removed to create this spacious, light-filled playroom.

OPPOSITE: The master bedroom.

20

HOUSE OF THE SEASONS

A common complaint against Texas is that it has no seasons or, put another way, the seasons never change. It's either sunny and mild or sunny and scorching hot. One cannot look out the window and see the brilliance of a New England autumn or even the icy blue of a snowy day, but Benjamin Epperson of Jefferson could have. When he built this Italianate house in 1872, the tower was glazed with floor-to-ceiling stained glass so that the change of the seasons could be had at the turn of a head. There was summer in a deep shady green, spring in a yellow-green, autumn in an orangey red, and winter so blue and cold you expected to see Dr. Zhivago crossing the lawn.

At some point after Epperson's time, the house, which is now a bed-and-breakfast, became known as the House of the Seasons. Painstakingly renovated by its owner, Richard Collins of Dallas, the house is as lovely as it is mysterious.

Epperson was at the end of a remarkable career in Texas politics when he, it appears, hired the well-known New York architect Arthur Gillman to design a house. Gillman's architectural credits were many and distinguished, including the Equitable Insurance Company's building, St. John's Church, and most of the capitol at Albany. But he was also

a visionary. Previously, as a Boston architect, he had argued passionately for the city to fill in the bay to create the Back Bay and the stylish Commonwealth Avenue, which was eventually carried out by the State. Did he, who might never have set foot in Texas, fashion the seasonable tower, or was this Epperson's idea?

The answer to that question may never be known, but it goes to the very heart of the house. It is essentially Greek Revival in plan, with rooms upstairs and downstairs arranged on either side of wide, gracious corridors. But where you would expect to find a staircase featured prominently in the lower corridor, the Epperson house leaves the Greek Revival behind in favor of an Italianate expression. In later Victorian Italianate houses, the tower would provide an asymmetrical vertical element, but here the excitement happens at the center of the hallway, with a view upward through a charming circular balustrade on the second floor beyond to a blue dome painted with allegorical figures bearing flowers, and upward further still into the lantern of the tower. The house seems to tease you upward, offering rewards at every level. The staircase is at the side of the corridor, announced by two hooded moldings. Under one arch

PREVIOUS PAGE: The colors in the lantern are believed to represent the seasons, hence the name of the house. From the windows pictured, one can see the lawn as it might appear in autumn (red-orange) or in winter (blue).

BELOW: Side elevation showing first- and second-story bay windows.

OVERLEAF: The front facade of the House of the Seasons. The house, with a formal Greek Revival plan of rooms arranged symmetrically along a central corridor, is graced with Italianate detailing and a tower that rises up out of the core of the house. Note how the arched upper windows seem to complete the lower windows.

is the pathway to an exterior door; beneath the other, the staircase begins its ascent. Moving upward from the second floor toward the lantern, the stairs are steeper, actually becoming vertiginous on the final rise to the tower.

Benjamin Epperson was lame in one leg (from a riding accident in his youth), and it is doubtful that he made the trip up to see the seasons change very often, though it is easy to imagine his three children delighting in it. But after moving in, there were upheavals in his life. His wife died the following year; he married again two years later to a very young woman (who would bear him two more children); and then, in 1878, he died in this house at the very young age of fifty-two.

Epperson had packed an amazing amount of accomplishments into that short life, and this house ably communicated not only his success, but his awareness of what was fashionable. An abridged account of his biography would have him being born in Mississippi, educated at Princeton, and in Texas practicing law in Clarksville and becoming elected to the office of county commissioner when he was himself still too young to vote. In 1847 (just two years after annexation), he was elected to the second state legislature; in 1859 he was one of four men called to consult with Governor Sam Houston concerning Abraham Lincoln's offer to send federal troops to Texas to help avoid secession. Like Houston, Epperson was an ardent Unionist, but he ran and was elected to the Confederate Congress, having been convinced that separation was inevitable. After the war, he was elected to the United States Congress. All the while he was practicing law and serving as president of the Memphis, El Paso, and Pacific Railroad Company.

He had lived in Clarksville as a practicing lawyer and in Austin and Washington as a statesman, but he chose Jefferson to build his fine, grand house, and that may be because Jefferson was a wealthy, bustling little city boasting the state's largest inland port. Cargo ships could navigate the Big Cypress River from New Orleans and Shreveport because of a logjam that made the water deep enough. Just after Epperson's house was finished, however, the logjam was blown up and with it the future of Jefferson. The following year, the rail line bypassed it, and Jefferson became a sleepy, forgotten little town filled with street after street of fine Greek Revival and Victorian homes.

Although the derelict homes and the curbless roadways with weeping willows shaking hands across the way give Jefferson a haunting Brigadoon-like air, Collins, who was enchanted by Jefferson as a boy, has devoted himself to the preservation of as many of the houses as possible. Since 1973 he has bought about twenty-five properties, including the House of the Seasons, to bring them back to life again. He says that architecture is all we have that we can see and touch of the lives of early settlers.

Certainly the House of the Seasons conjures thoughts of Benjamin Epperson. What if Epperson had lived in Texas long enough to know that the seasons actually do change (albeit subtly) and the windows in the tower weren't about the seasons at all, but rather about the times of the day? What if Benjamin Epperson lived out his last few years simply delighting in the beams of colored light that wafted down through the lantern into the heart of his home?

BELOW: The dome, which illustrates allegorical scenes of unknown origins. This dome rises above the second floor and is not visible from the outside.

OPPOSITE: The circular opening in the second floor, ringed with a balustrade, is aligned with the dome so that the dome and the lantern above it can be viewed from the first floor. Beyond, the central window and sill disguise a door to the front balcony.

OPPOSITE: The first- and second-floor corridors looking toward the back entrances of the house.

BELOW: The formal dining room. This room and all others throughout the house are appointed with late nineteenth-century antiques.

BELOW: The master bedroom with its decorative red panes in the bay window.

OPPOSITE: The blue bedroom, sometimes called the child's room, is one of three upstairs bedrooms. Archival photographs provide evidence that Epperson himself slept downstairs in a room used—and clearly designed as—a formal parlor.

OVERLEAF: The formal parlor with original nineteenth-century chairs and settee. The current owner of the House of the Seasons, Richard Collins, traced Epperson's daughter, Ada, to Oklahoma, where he was able to purchase the furniture now in this room from her son, Benjamin Epperson III.

34

LEAGUE HOUSE

"A profound sense of sorrow seemed to cast itself over those assembled in various places in Galveston last night when word was passed that Mr. League was dead." So concluded the *Galveston Daily News'* obituary of J.C. League, "the millionaire pioneer" who died at his home on January 13, 1916. The funeral was to be held from the family residence at 10:30 the following day.

It went without saying in the local newspaper that the family residence, this home on Broadway, would be spacious enough to accommodate the sizable number of mourners that could be expected to pay their respects to the prominent, beloved Mr. League, who had been born on the island in 1849. Having made a fortune in real estate (his gift of land established the neighboring community of League City), League was dedicated to improving Galveston, which manifested itself in dozens of civic venues, and in discreet, personal ways too. He was known to make quiet gifts of money to help those rendered destitute by the hurricanes that had ravaged the island in 1900 and again in 1915. Sadly, one of those to seek and receive such help, just a week before League's death, was none other than the architect of his grand house—Nicholas Clayton—who, more than any one person, gave shape to the city of Galveston, assuring with his skill a prominence that would far outlive the city's thriving business life.

Clayton was seventy-six when League gave him $250, the first installment of a loan for $1,000, to help repair his family home, badly damaged by the storm of 1915. His own death was to follow shortly after that of his patron, following an accident he had while trying to repair the fireplace in this house. But in his heyday, Clayton was one of the most prolific and prosperous architects in the history of Texas. In fact, according to his advertisements, he was the first established professional architect in Texas. Buildings in Texas—Dallas, Austin, Waco, Houston—Louisiana, and Florida survive as cherished monuments in their respective locations. It is true that the commissions that took him away from home were monumental by nature—churches, schools, and the occasional commercial building—and that is because Galveston was an extraordinary, three-dimensional portfolio of just such jobs.

In his prime, he dominated the architectural commissions in the city, winning dozens of prestigious jobs, which included St. Mary's Cathedral, Trinity Church, the University of Texas Medical School, the highly decorative Ursuline Academy (now demolished), and exquisitely detailed Victorian office buildings on and off the commercial district known as the Strand. But in Galveston he also designed homes, and had Galveston not suffered the mid-twentieth-century

PREVIOUS SPREAD: View of Clayton's three-story League house from across Galveston's Broadway Boulevard, situated amid palms and palmettos.

OPPOSITE: The porte cochere accommodates a driveway through the grounds and accentuates the house's deep porch. In contrast to the verticality of Victorian design, the porte cochere gives the League house a wider, more horizontal appearance.

purges inflicted on most American cities, its Broadway Boulevard would have placed the League house alongside other Clayton-designed homes.

As it is, there is one other surviving mansion on Broadway, undoubtedly the best-known house that, for all its glamour, sets in relief the quieter pleasures of the League house. The Gresham house (now known as the Bishop's Palace, for the bishop who lived there for many years) demonstrates how adept Clayton was in following and personalizing the prevalent fashions of the day—in this case, the Romanesque, popularized by Boston's H. H. Richardson. The Gresham house is a highly rusticated three-story house made of brick that is faced with rough-cut granite, limestone, and sandstone. Its roof is a busy composition of gables and chimney towers all dominated by the three-story cylindrical tower that endows the facade with the kind of asymmetry that links it with the less flamboyant Victorian residences of its time. Sited close to the street on its corner lot, the house assumes an urban aspect, existing as a showcase for Gresham's wealth and Clayton's skill. The architect was quoted as saying, "The majesty of expression conveyed by the castellated effects of the picturesque stone walls . . . recall to the traveled of our community the stately mansions of England and the chateaux of France."

Just as the Gresham house was nearing completion, John Charles League and his wife, the former Nellie Ball (daughter of George Ball, a prominent banker and philanthropist), hired Nicholas Clayton to design their family home. On September 24, 1892, Clayton noted in his diary that he had sent Mr. League the floor plans of the house and three elevations. Curiously, the floor plan of the first floor was close to identical to that of the Gresham house, minus a music room. Both houses were entered centrally up a high stoop and across a generous porch. Each possessed a vestibule, which gave way to an entrance hall on axis with the stairwell. Each was endowed with a parlor on the left of the hall and a library, followed by a dining room, on the right of the hall. There, however, is where the similarities ended.

Like the man himself, who was wont to give his money anonymously (a trait he shared with his father-in-law), the house developed in such a way as to belie League's great wealth. It was stately, to be sure, but the articulation of its wide, shuttered exterior had little to do with a display of material wealth. Its spirit was understated. Like the Leagues, it was generous and approachable, comfortable in its surroundings.

The fabric of the building was concrete, scored to imitate cut stone on the body of the house, and sculpted to resemble rusticated stone on the quoins and the arched basement surround. At the entrance door, pilasters continued in concrete the classical details of the front porch, where wooden columns with Doric capitals and turned balusters betrayed Clayton's Colonial Revival treatment of the Leagues' house. Instead of a turret or otherwise dramatic, vertical element, this facade had a different visual interest—a lovely porte cochere connected to the porch on one end of a staircase, and the landscape of palmettos and palms on the other.

Clayton never returned to the Colonial Revival style, though there is every reason to believe it was a success. He remained friendly with Mr. League for the next twenty years—possibly naming his son, John Charles, born in 1901, after his admirable client.

He had given the Leagues, both true children of the Island, a house that belonged in Galveston. Although one cannot see the ocean from its porch, the sense of it is palpable. It's only blocks away. And the big, wide Broadway will take you there.

LEFT: Fluted columns with Ionic capitals frame the staircase with its broad, curved landing offering ascent. A newel post carved like a lantern marks the pivot of the main steps. At the next landing, a stained-glass window depicts ivy, which seems to dangle behind diamond-shaped panes.

BELOW: Dining room with a Clayton-designed sideboard on the left and his decorative beamed ceiling above.

BOTTOM: This semicircular bay window in the parlor echoes the circular sweep of the wide porch. Such gracious forms depart from the more typical angular lines of Clayton's structures.

OVERLEAF: The library, denoted "sitting room" in Clayton's plans, offers a corner view of the porte cochere.

42

TROST HOUSE

As the century turned from the nineteenth to the twentieth, the pass to the North—El Paso—was, as the name implies, the place that best accommodated overland travel from Mexico to Texas and then northward into New Mexico and westward to California. It seems everyone—Apache marauders, Mexican bandits, flamboyant outlaws, garden-variety ruffians, and cattle rustlers—was just passing through, as rootless as the trains that whistled by. But in the midst of this rough culture, there began to grow up a small community of citizens (four thousand in 1890) who saw greater economic opportunities in the location, or felt the allure of the cool desert landscape where the lower Rockies meet the Rio Grande. Some felt the draw of Mexico, with its rich Spanish traditions, just beyond a still-blurry borderline. El Paso, the frontier outpost, was ripe for an architect who could give form and character to these myriad influences and reflect back to the small community a sense of itself as a great, burgeoning southwestern city.

But Henry Trost, who was to assume that role in the life of the city and the Southwest in general, was, it would seem, taking a long time getting there. His brother Gustavus was already in El Paso practicing architecture in 1902,

but Henry, the designer, chose a much more circuitous route from the family home in Toledo, Ohio, making stops along the way that would inevitably shape his sensibility. By the time he arrived in 1903 at the age of thirty-nine, Trost had opened practices in a handful of western towns, including Colorado Springs, Pueblo, and Tucson. He had also explored Texas, finding Dallas to be "nothing more than a country town," although, farther south, in the booming port city of Galveston, Nicholas Clayton, one of the most sought-after architects in the state, gave him a job in his busy office. Trost held it for about a year and then moved on again—this time to Dodge City, where he and a friend opened up a firm.

Trost was restless, searching, and when he left Dodge a year later, he made a decisive move to Chicago, the city that had been a point of reference for him since his youth. He was to stay eight years in the city (from 1888 to 1896), at precisely the moment developments in architectural technique and thought were beginning to reshape the way Americans built. William Le Baron Jenney was building skyscrapers using his steel-frame construction, Bostonian H. H. Richardson was just completing his revolutionary Marshall Field's Department Store, and others, in what was being called the

THE ATMOSPHERE OF THE SOUTHWEST IS WONDERFULLY CLEAR. THE MOUNTAIN MASSES ARE RUGGED AND THEIR SHADOWS AND CONTRASTS ARE SHARPLY DEFINED. THE SUNSET TINTS ARE PRIMARY COLORS, ILLUMINATED WITH WONDERFUL GOLD AND PURPLE. THE HORIZONS ARE INFINITE—LONG, DISTANT LEVEL LINES, BROKEN ONLY BY THE FAR-OFF MOUNTAINS OR THE SCRUBBY DESERT VEGETATION AGAINST THE SKY.

—FROM A BROCHURE FOR TROST & TROST

Chicago School, were building towers of pure architectural beauty, devoid of ornamentation.

At the heart of this frenzy was the masterful Louis Sullivan, who did not believe that absence of ornament made a building modern; it was the handling and composition of the abstract geometric forms of architecture that did. And ornament, in his hands inspired by nature (not history), was never applied after the fact, but grew naturally, organically out of the overall concerns of the architecture. It was his role as a proponent of ornament, in fact, that must have brought Trost to Sullivan's attention: A contest for ornament design judged by Sullivan, among others, had awarded Trost a second-place medal for his drawing of a (very Sullivanesque) iron gate.

In words and in built designs, Sullivan promulgated a new, modern way of creating architecture, which drew dozens of talented architects to his firm, among them, convincing evidence suggests, Henry Trost. Those who had long been under the spell of Sullivan's lessons had already begun to create homes that in their number and in their similar attitude to architectural mass constituted the first truly Modern American style. Frank Lloyd Wright related these ground-hugging forms to the prairie—hence the label Prairie Style. But the style was not as prescriptive as Wright's term suggests, and when it began to spread outward into the American landscape, the notion of the prairie was misleading; it was modernity and cutting-edge fashion that clients saw in it.

Such was not the case in El Paso when Trost arrived in 1903. He was quick to receive large and impressive commissions—the Neoclassical house for a millionaire (which became the Museum of Art) and a Mission Revival house, where Pancho Villa would soon meet with U.S. authorities in an effort to quell border violence. Not until 1909 did Trost

have the opportunity to give his sensibility full play—in his own $15,000 home.

At the crest of a hillside with a commanding view into Mexico to the south and the old city of El Paso to the east, the house rose up from the street like a cathedral. The facade was distinguished by two tall planters, two door-height columns with ornamented capitals, and two concrete planters emphasizing the terrace of the brick porch. The double-height porch stretches to meet a gable roof that extends, in every direction, far beyond the actual structure of the house. The underside of the deep eaves, like the ornament that parallels the lines of the gable just beneath it, is a cream-colored stucco, as are the sections of the facade supporting windows and lightening the heft of the brick base.

Because the house occupies a corner lot, the side facade is equally commanding. Another towering gable roof overhanging the gable-shaped ornament and window design beneath echoes the front facade. A smaller gable roof hovering over a bricked arched opening beckons the visitor up the stair stoop to the enclosed porch and entrance door. Stretching along the side of this western elevation are sections of ornamented stucco that form the exterior walls of an upstairs balcony. Supported by brick columns below, the balcony offers further shade to the living space inside.

The outside is bathed in bright southwestern light, unabated by shade trees. Once inside and up three steps from the foyer, it is possible to appreciate the functional aspects of the overarching roofs and the heavy brick massing. It is dark, but the contrast only serves to dramatize the way one experiences the interior. Even though Trost has conceived of the core of the house as one long, open space bound by ceiling beams that cross from living room to dining room, the spaces unfold slowly. Trost's ornamental frieze of yucca, thistles, and palms that runs the perimeter of these

joined spaces and into the fireplace niche between them can only be examined when one's eyes have become acclimated to the dim coolness within.

In their prolific practice, Trost, with brothers Adolphus and Gustavus and nephew George Trost, left a decisive mark on the architecture of the Southwest. Although he would allude to the Prairie Style in many subsequent buildings, he was never able to re-create the scale and magnificence of his own home. But El Paso and its arid, desertlike environment seemed never to lose its allure. Thus, it seems only fitting that when he died at age seventy-three, he was found seated on the front porch of his house, facing his beloved desert city.

LEFT: The dining room looking toward the living room. A series of rafters, corbels, and piers mask the difference in size between the two rooms. Furniture and light fixtures in both rooms were designed by Trost.

BELOW: A closer view of the living room. The stained-glass doors at the far end lead to the front balcony. Barely detectable on the wall plates just below the ceiling and surrounding both rooms are the stencils of a frieze depicting thistles, palms, and cacti.

BELOW: Steps lead downward from the foyer (at left) to Trost's office, a half-story lower. Not visible are the clerestory windows in the study that provide backlighting to stained-glass windows in the dining room. A short span of steps (at center) lead up into the core of the house, the second level of this split-level house.

OPPOSITE: The core of the house culminates at the stained-glass windows in the doors leading out to the south balcony. The Prairie Style in Texas has adapted to the flora of the Southwest as seen in the frieze of thistle, cacti, and palms above the door, as well as in the windows, which are embellished with highly stylized stained-glass thistles.

HOGG HOUSE

When Atlee Ayres was six years old, his family moved to San Antonio and settled into a dwelling immediately across the plaza from the Alamo. In 1880, the battle to occupy that structure was still in living memory, as was Texas independence in 1836 and statehood in 1845. But the drama of the events that extricated San Antonio from Mexico hardly erased the very deep imprint that Spanish culture—the first Mass was held in 1692—had left on the city and its environs. Remnants of Spanish buildings—the missions, the Governor's Palace, and other, more humble abodes—were available everywhere for the aesthetically minded Ayres.

It is difficult, however, to see the familiar in a new light, and for the impressionable Ayres it was not home that defined his sensibility but New York, where he studied architecture at the Metropolitan School of Art. Eclecticism was the order of the day, and when he returned to San Antonio in 1898 to set up a practice, he offered clients an assortment of styles—Colonial Revival, Mission, Prairie, Tudor Revival, Arts and Crafts, and Italian Renaissance—and proceeded to embellish the city with some of its best residences.

He would remain flexible in regard to style throughout his career, but in 1918, following a vacation to Southern California, he fell in love with the Spanish Revival style. It was such a strong epiphany that he wanted to move there and join the other practitioners. The dream persisted for several years, during which time he began to appreciate (seemingly for the first time) that San Antonio had the same Spanish heritage as California and that the style would be just as at home there.

Of the handful of Spanish Revival houses that pepper the affluent neighborhood of San Antonio's Olmos Park, the house for Thomas and Marie Hogg, designed in 1923 and completed in 1924, stands out. Thomas Hogg was the youngest son of the former governor of Texas, James Hogg, and the brother of distinguished siblings, who had made Houston their home—older brother and de facto head of the family Will, sister Ima, and lawyer and Will's partner Mike. (See page 90 for more about the Hoggs.) In 1919 oil had been discovered on the family plantation in East Texas, providing fodder for Thomas and Marie's rather carefree lifestyle of breeding horses and raising dogs.

The couple arrived in San Antonio in 1920, and by 1924 Will Hogg was writing to his sister-in-law, exhorting her and Tom to live within their means. "Suppress your Rolls-Royce

PREVIOUS PAGE: The back door of the Hogg house, flanked by Moorish spiraling columns, reveals a view through the entrance corridor to the front lawn. Both openings are complemented with decorative wrought-iron gates. The circular fountain (here used as a planter) was a feature Ayres appreciated in Mexican architecture.

BELOW: The less formal house plan, which angles into the property, was a clear break from Ayres's square-planned Italian-style villas. The relaxed plan and the gardens of the Hogg house suggest a more intimate connection with nature.

vanities," he wrote, "until we can ascertain our real financial worth." But by then, Atlee Ayres was just putting the finishing touches on the Hoggs' Spanish Revival house, which was to cost $153,000. After his travels in California, Ayres had infused several modest homes with the spirit of the Spanish Revival, but the Hogg house was his first opportunity to illustrate on a large scale and with an ample budget his understanding of the features that made the best Spanish Revival homes so picturesque. For instance, the Hogg house plan departed strikingly from plans for the Mediterranean houses he had designed under the influence of the Italian Renaissance. Rather than a formal, ordered block formation, Ayres bent the plan so that a wing of the house angled deeper into the house site, helping to embrace a patio on the backside. The calculated spin-off of this decision was reflected on the front exterior in the variety of shapes that carry the house into the lot—a protruding double-height square with an irregular assortment of windows meets a receding rectangular space with three pairs of ground-level French doors, which, in turn, abut a circular tower with a second-level balcony. The effect is that of a picturesque village of independent structures that have somehow mysteriously been conjoined. Indeed, the tower appears so sculpturally in the round that it is hard to grasp how it connects to the house at all.

Once beyond a decorative wrought iron gate and a massive door, a reception room with a shallow barrel vault spans the depth of the house and points the eye directly ahead through another decorative iron gate to the flagstone patio outside. A carved, circular planter (what Ayres intended to be a fountain) brings a splash of bright color to the dark tile floor. This room is the key to the interior plan. Left of it and down two steps is a small book-lined study and a formal living room. Right, beyond the self-contained stair tower, the asymmetry of the plan becomes apparent. Just at the end of the room, one sees the patterns of the floor tile altering and the ceiling moldings shaping out a triangular space that shifts the axis to accommodate a formal dining room, and, adjacent to it—through another iron gate—a curious corridor, what Ayres called "the cloister," that follows the angles noticed on the exterior.

The very notion of a cloister implies privacy, specifically the confined interior gardens of monastic structures, whose pleasures were vouchsafed only to the dwellers. The iron door, like those to the front and back doors, implies a separation from the interior space, and indeed, the cloister could be thought of as a different realm—a passageway that allowed servants to move quietly from the butler's pantry or back staircase into the dining room that opens onto it. A powder room at the end of it and a niche formerly for the telephone further imply its functional role. But the beauty of this space is the way it buffers the interior of the house from direct exposure to the outside world while ushering in generous supplies of light and greenery. Ayres may have called it a cloister, but he had no intention of hiding it away.

Ayres was a serious student of architecture who tirelessly put together a voluminous library of books on the subject. He was an inveterate traveler, touring Spain to study farmhouses and, following the completion of the Hogg house, Mexico to photograph architecture for a book that was published in 1926. But in the end, it is not Spain or Mexico that one perceives in the Hogg house, but California. What he saw of the Spanish Revival there affected him deeply and showed him the way to give back part of San Antonio's cultural legacy. That he did it so well and so inventively is his architectural legacy.

OPPOSITE: The spiral staircase winds its way sensuously up the cylindrical tower. The iron window opens into what Ayres called "the cloister," a hallway that flanked the dining room and provided a light-filled buffer between the outdoors and the interior.

BELOW: The play of hand-troweled plaster across the chimney and walls: The ribbons and shield are in high relief along the mantel face, and the sculptural vaults are in deep relief where the wall meets the ceiling.

LEFT: Guests step down into the living room from the entrance hall and can pass through to the now enclosed loggia, glimpsed through the open doorway at the far end. Ayres sent Mrs. Hogg to California to select the dark cordovan tiles seen on the floor from the same craftsman employed by his Spanish Revival mentors there. The patterns change five times across the first floor.

BELOW: A very shallow barrel vault, springing from a decorative plaster molding, gently arches over the entrance hall. Here the view is through the gate leading into the back garden.

BOTTOM: Here, where Ayres's cloister (beyond the opened gate) and the dining room open onto the entrance hall, the axis of the house shifts. The cloister follows the angle of the house plan, which embraces the backyard and patio.

2

STIRRINGS
OF PLACE:
THE ROMANTIC
AND PRACTICAL

Courtyard of the Drane-Cook house.

ARMSTRONG-FERGUSON HOUSE

Spanish Revival and Mission Revival were styles that had a natural affinity for San Antonio and its environs. The smooth stucco and imaginative forms of an Atlee Ayres house (page 50) or the reiterated parapet of the Alamo at the King Ranch (page 68)—these are the aesthetic expressions the Spaniards left behind. But there was another influence built into the architecture of Spain—one that is sometimes overlooked. It was derived from the Moors, who occupied Spain from 711 to circa 1492, leaving behind structures and decorative surfaces of remarkable intricacy and beauty. By the time the Spaniards arrived in the Southwest, those forms had been thoroughly assimilated into their own building vocabulary, emerging without fanfare in the occasional keyhole window or, for instance, in the spiraling doorway columns of the Alamo.

In America, Moorish style had a brief fifteen minutes of fame in the mid-nineteenth-century romantic fascination with the exotic. P. T. Barnum's Iranistan in Connecticut, was an over-the-top example, as was Frederic Edwin Church's home, Olana, on the banks of the Hudson. But in San Antonio, the style was not revisited until the arrival of architect Harvey Lindsay Page in 1899.

It is not clear why Page moved to San Antonio. His roots were deep in Washington, D.C., where his father, Charles Grafton Page, was celebrated as the inventor of the induction coil and the circuit breaker. Page was born there on January 9, 1859, and, after attending Andover, he returned to the city, matriculating at the Emerson Institute and working for J. L. Smithmeyer, the architect of the National Library. On his own, he designed the Army and Navy Club, the Metropolitan Club, and the Phoebe Hearst home.

As early as 1907, in San Antonio, he was designing a spectacular depot for the International Great Northern railway, combining Mission elements and Moorish details. Here, however, Mission parapets are quite overwhelmed by a massive dome with a circular lantern and towers rising up from each of the four corners. Broad, arched openings and a decorative quatrefoil in the parapet seem to turn the depot into a kind of Islamic shrine.

Several years later, he designed the home on the following pages, which is now owned by architect Ted Flato of the firm Lake/Flato (see page 212) and his wife, Katy. The house is a refuge, completely hidden from the suburban street by a lush garden of palmettos and banana trees, under a canopy

PREVIOUS PAGE: View from the garden toward the back facade. Colonel Armstrong, one of the earliest residents of the home, hired homeless drifters to build the low stone wall that surrounds the property. He, like his successors, greatly valued the shaded privacy of the house.

BELOW: The arched front door flanked by keyhole-shaped openings has again become the front door into the home. It leads into the Moorish garden room, the enchanted heart of the house, which had been marginalized by previous owners.

OVERLEAF: The room that won the hearts of current owners Ted and Katy Flato and influenced the restoration of the Craftsman-style house by inspiring an openness to nature. Flato punched a giant skylight into the center of the roof and turned the room into the family's primary gathering place.

of enormous old live oaks that gesticulate so freely and happily that they seem to dominate the quieter house. But the house now rises to the occasion, thanks to the efforts of the Flatos.

When they first encountered it, the entrance was along the driveway into the property, through a side door. The kitchen had almost no access to the outdoors, and the primary feature of the house, a great square room abounding with Moorish details, had been virtually marginalized. It had all the makings of an entrance room: Small keyhole arches suggesting the exotic realm beyond flanked the great door leading into it. Inside, wide arches enclosing casement windows spanned the two exterior walls on either side of the door, and the wood between them was carved with stylized arabesques drawn from nature. There were spiraling columns that supported moldings around the arches and iron mullioned circles of thick glass crowning the windows inside the arches. But the house, sadly, had been sorely neglected and misunderstood.

Describing when he first saw the house, Flato says, "I loved it. It was a patient that needed healing. I could feel it." It is always interesting when one architect lives in another architect's home, and Flato, in fact, refers to their remodeling as a "collaboration with Page."

Among the most important treatments on the way to healing the house was to open it to the beauty of its surroundings. The Moorish room reclaimed its status as the front room, entered from a refashioned stoop of what Flato calls "textured stucco, of the sort you might see in Andalusia." The approach to this door leads you through the sylvan, fern-filled, mossy garden beneath the mighty oak's winding boughs. Flato, in true Moroccan style, turned this great room into a courtyard by punching through the roof to give it a vast skylight. The natural light that now streams in nurtures the potted plants and filters into the adjacent study and the more formal living room.

For reasons unknown—lack of money or lack of nerve—the Moorish style is confined to this one room. From that point onward, the house becomes Craftsman, which in 1909 was, after all, the cutting edge of architecture. To see the simple, ordered beauty of the living room, dining room, and wide staircase and hallway is to observe Page's easy transition from flourishing, curving lines to the tighter compositions of wooden form and exposed construction.

The Flatos have honored the change in tone, even enhancing it by way of reusing aspects of the original house. It occurs in the decorative wooden cross-hatching on doors, cabinets, and window screens, which Flato noticed on a few surviving details and replicated in new additions. The glass-faced kitchen cabinets supported by Craftsman-like brackets have been resurrected in the modernized kitchen. On the exterior, Flato copied the huge brackets Page designed to support his six-foot-deep eaves shading the house. Then Flato did something wonderfully counter to the more inward-looking design of the original house. Taking advantage of the shifting grade of the site, which gave the house a split level, he opened the kitchen to a balcony that extends out into their shady garden.

Flato calls his house a hybrid, for its melding of the nuts and bolts of the Craftsman style with the exotic, fanciful Moorish idiom of the entrance. This one room has so enchanted the family that last year they took a vacation to Morocco. Says Flato, "We went to find our roots."

LEFT: The kitchen in the original house cast a blind eye to the lush landscape outdoors. In his restoration, Flato opened the space to a covered balcony set upon the rooftop that covers a carport below. The new brackets emulate those supporting the eaves of the house, which are by Harvey Page.

BELOW: The Craftsman stairwell occupies a wide hallway, which in an earlier incarnation was the entrance corridor. Previous owners entered the house where the large window on the right is now.

BOTTOM: With dark brown paint covering Harvey Page's Craftsman details, the Flatos put in relief the window surrounds, fireplace, and moldings. The cross-hatching on the screens was a Page detail that Flato reiterated in the doors and windows he added.

KING RANCH

In some basic sense, the romance of Henrietta Chamberlain King's first home, the jacal, seems never to have left her, even in the building of two subsequent ranch homes—the first, a plantation-style house above the creek Santa Gertrudis (hence the name of the home, and later, a new breed of cattle) and the second, the grand home pictured on these pages. Although she was the well-educated, pious daughter of a Presbyterian missionary, she took immediately to the life of her rough-and-tumble husband, Captain Richard King, gamely embracing its hardships and remoteness. And even in prosperity, within the magnificent confines of this home—so like a crusader's castle out on the Wild Horse Desert of South Texas—she managed to offer her family and friends the comfort and informality of that blanket beneath the mesquite.

The site of the house was recommended by the Kings' friend (at that time Lt. Colonel) Robert E. Lee, who was stationed in Texas from 1856 to 1861. Lee was a frequent guest, who dined with them, according to Mrs. King, on their humble tin plates. On one such visit Lee gave Captain King a fateful bit of advice: "Buy land," he said, "and never sell."

And so King bought land—a lot of land. By the time of his death in 1885, he owned more than 600,000 acres of Texas ranch land. By the time Henrietta died in 1925, King Ranch was almost as large as the state of Rhode Island, stretching along the Gulf of Mexico for more than one hundred miles. Cattle and quarter horses were acquired on an equally vast scale; crops were produced; and, in time, oil was pumped. Henrietta King had become the matriarch of an empire.

During her marriage to Captain King, she was a partner in their business affairs, and following his death she was a capable manager, but in 1886 she hired Robert Kleberg to be the business administrator of the ranch. Kleberg (see Knights' Gambit, page 200) had inspired the admiration of Captain King when he argued a case against the rancher and ably won it for his client, and at the time of his hiring, he was engaged to the Kings' daughter, Alice. Kleberg helped bring to fruition many of Henrietta's dreams, one of which was the acquisition of all the amenities necessary—train lines, electricity, water, lumber, financing, churches, even a newspaper—to build the small community of Kingsville. He was certainly by her side in 1915 when King Ranch was

WHEN I CAME TO TEXAS AS A BRIDE IN 1854, THE LITTLE RANCH HOME, THEN A MERE JACAL,
AS MEXICANS WOULD CALL IT, WAS OUR ABODE FOR MANY MONTHS UNTIL OUR MAIN RANCH DWELLING
WAS COMPLETED. BUT I DOUBT IF IT FALLS TO THE LOT OF ANY BRIDE TO HAVE HAD SO HAPPY A
HONEYMOON. ON HORSEBACK WE ROAMED THE BROAD PRAIRIES. WHEN I GREW TIRED MY HUSBAND
WOULD SPREAD A MEXICAN BLANKET FOR ME AND THEN I WOULD TAKE MY SIESTA UNDER THE SHADE
OF THE MESQUITE TREE.

—FROM THE DIARIES OF HENRIETTA CHAMBERLAIN KING

PREVOIUS SPREAD: Keyhole arches and the small parapets at the roofline suggest the Mission Revival style. Henrietta King was a surprisingly modest woman, and while the informality of the house reflects that characteristic, the scale of the house is immense, an aspect that is particularly striking when viewed from the wide-open grasslands of the ranch.

OPPOSITE: The central courtyard around which the house takes shape. Business partners and lawyers were put up in private rooms accessible across the courtyard but discrete from the family quarters. The spectacular stained-glass windows, which are two stories high and illuminate the stairwell inside, were designed by Tiffany & Co.

OVERLEAF: When not hosting elegant dinner parties at their fifty-seat table, this dining room is the locus of informal family gatherings. It is filled with the trophies and photographs of their renowned thoroughbreds' victories—Assault won the Triple Crown, and his half-brother, Bold Venture, won the Kentucky Derby and Belmont races.

envisioned and built (1912–1915), although she seems to have been the final authority on every decision. Following Henrietta's death, Robert and Alice Kleberg and their children after them would be at the helm of King Ranch.

The family solicited ideas for the ranch house design from a number of architects before deciding on the San Antonio firm of Adams and Adams, which had furnished them with a drawing of a house in the Mission Revival style. The Alamo may have been a point of reference—even now a large painting of it fills the wall above the fireplace in the living room (noted on the plans as the "grand salon"), and a carriage house bears the great parapets of the heroic structure. But for all its glory, the Alamo was, after all, merely the surviving chapel of a working mission. At King Ranch, Mission Revival was taken at face value: Like a traditional mission, where working families lived around an interior courtyard, so dozens of King family members were to be accommodated (albeit far more handsomely) upstairs, in bedrooms that opened to a wide hallway that lined the courtyard and opened broadly to it through a series of arches, which were later closed in with glass. Many of these rooms are now endowed with attached sleeping porches.

The public rooms of the house follow the same plan, although the hallway of the upstairs becomes an open loggia for the first floor, giving the rooms—the long, barrel-vaulted living room, a dining room on the western edge, and bedrooms for business partners (discrete from the family's sleeping quarters) on the southern side—direct exposure to the courtyard. The northwestern corner of the plan accommodates a book-filled library, and the northeastern corner functioned as Robert Kleberg's office.

Outside of his office, the broad entrance hall brings together the sometimes rough realities of ranch life with the delicacy and refinement of ornamentation. For instance, just beyond the framed skin of a rattlesnake one sees the ornate ironwork of a Tiffany's iron balustrade. And as one follows the stained-glass windows (also Tiffany's) rising upward to the second floor, there are, opposite, the beloved Santa Gertrudis and Longhorn bull heads.

Apparently, the Klebergs worked closely with Tiffany Studios to capture their sense of how one should live in the hot climate of South Texas. Archival photos show natural-wicker furniture in the living room—now, in white, carving out a sitting area in an upstairs hallway. Most of the floors are either stone or tile, reflecting Mrs. King's hope that no man coming in off the ranch with muddy boots would feel uncomfortable in the confines of the home. Even the dining room, with its Mission table that seats fifty and which has been the setting for parties welcoming presidents and generals and foreign dignitaries, has the formality born of its immense scale and the extravagant elegance of the Kings' dinner settings and meals. However, its blue-tile wainscoting and photographs of prizewinning horses raised at the ranch assure that it is the kind of room where family members can relax and feel comfortable in every-day life.

A bit of family humor, probably generated by Robert Kleberg, has it that if Captain King came back to the ranch, the only thing he'd recognize would be his lovely wife. But there's also reason to believe he would see her hand immediately in the design of the ranch house. As the *San Antonio Express* reported in 1915: "She wanted this house to express in its architecture her very own conception of Texas and life—to be a work of art expressing the soul of things . . ." Hers was not a pretentious sensibility; rather it was that of one who knew how to live on the land, valuing the way of life that she had shared with King and their many descendants.

BELOW: The sleeping porch adjacent to Henrietta King's bedroom. It is typical of the sleeping porches attached to almost all of the rooms lining the halls of the second floor and overlooking the courtyard.

BOTTOM: Henrietta King's bedroom.

RIGHT: A wide second-floor hallway, which acts as a buffer between the courtyard and the bedrooms. It accommodates the antique wicker furniture, seen here painted white, which was original to the house and can be seen, unpainted, in archival photographs of the living room.

OVERLEAF: While the formal entrance to the house is to the left just past the second column, this hallway acts as the primary pathway into the principal rooms of the house. Heads of the King family's favorite bulls, along with a few stags, adorn the walls. The staircase at right splits about midway up, turning left to the bedrooms and right toward the master bedroom suite.

DRANE-COOK HOUSE

Texas's first architecture—that is to say, the indigenous frontier structures of early settlers—found its most loyal and vocal advocate in the figure of architect David Williams (1890–1962). So ardent and dedicated was his study of the values inherent in early Texas building and so irresistible was he as a teacher and mentor that his influence on architects persists to this very day. One can trace his lineage easily through three generations—from O'Neil Ford and Arch Swank to Frank Welch, down to Max Levy, Natalye Appel, David Lake, Ted Flato, and Paul Lamb, to name only those architects represented in this book. Williams's influence was the fulcrum on which Texas architecture turned—from the houses in which style had become paramount to the houses in which place was paramount. He made it acceptable (almost imperative) to glance over one's shoulder to the past to remember what was elemental and appropriate for the landscape.

On the face of it, his was an unlikely sensibility to inspire such interest in the frontier: urbane and dapper, well-connected, well-traveled, and such a bon vivant that his studio in the conservative city of Dallas became the locus of a most bohemian coterie of friends and fellow artists. But

beneath the legendary panache of the man lay the memories of the boy who grew up in a dugout on the Panhandle Plains of Texas. Out under the big Texas sky his ideas had taken shape, and no amount of education or wealth or cultivation could shake off his lifelong love of the open range and the mythic symbols of early Texas—the romantic cowboy, the lone star, the ingenious cattle brand, the humble farm dwelling.

He found his way to engineering school at the University of Texas and specialized in architecture. But what stands out from this period is the college yearbook that he edited, illustrated, and dedicated to the state of Texas. The introductory page pictured his drawing of a cowboy on horseback gazing beyond at a vast landscape, followed by his grandiloquent language extolling Texas's virtues. The panegyric ended, in epic fashion, with this alluring invitation to turn the page: "The gate is down, ride thru." Some years later these words would be echoed in the opportunity to design the house on the following pages. But he was still young and restless in 1916, and when he saw a flyer advertising an engineering job in Tampico, he dropped out of school (one month before graduation), caught a steamer, and headed south. By the

A LOGICAL REGIONAL ARCHITECTURE HAS FOR ITS ORIGIN THE SIMPLE, EARLY FORMS OF BUILDING NATIVE TO ITS OWN LOCALE, AND GROWS BY PURELY FUNCTIONAL METHODS INTO AN INDIGENOUS FORM OF ART.

—DAVID WILLIAMS

time he left Mexico, he had become a relatively wealthy man, having earned enough money to fund extensive European travels and a life in New York City among the intellectuals of Washington Square.

When he returned home in 1923, his ardor for Texas had not abated; on the contrary, it had grown. He opened a Dallas office and soon gained a reputation as a talented designer. By the late 1920s he was traveling the state with his protégé O'Neil Ford, searching for prototypical frontier structures on which to build a new Texas style. The duo photographed humble dwellings, chronicling their shallow gabled metal roofs, stone structures, front porches, and decorative detailing with an eye toward distilling from them what was best. Writing for *The Southwestern Review*, Williams said, "It is better to throw away our habit of supposing everything beautiful in Texas had a foreign origin and to admit that these little houses are not French or Spanish or even English at all, but are natural, Texas art suited to our climate and indigenous to our soil."

Just as these thoughts were being recorded and the photos were being snapped—when, in fact, ideas of a Texas style were at their most thrilling—Williams received the largest commission of his career. It was for a grand house to be sited on the range of a fifty-acre ranch outside the small town of Corsicana. The clients, Frank Drane and his wife, wanted a pseudo-Spanish house of the sort they had seen in Florida, but they acceded to Williams's desire to do a Texas house. Thus he found himself facing a wide-open Texas landscape, and the "gate was down."

As Williams described it, "Mr. Drane charged me, when first we began its planning, to build this house to stand a thousand years as a monument to the Dranes. He further bade me to help him conjure up every conceivable thing that might be invented that could add to man's health, comfort,

happiness, and pleasure down the years." As it turned out, two generations were to call the house home, but the pleasure of seeing the house now is owing to the painstaking renovation it has received from Kay and Byron Cook, who stepped in to save it well before the thousand-year mark.

Thanks to their efforts, it is possible to see how Williams followed up on Drane's directive, with architectural design that fostered the kind of comfort Drane desired. For instance, air ventilation was ensured by the plan: One long hallway runs the length of the house from the front door to the highly decorative back door; and public rooms across the front of the house open widely to the incoming breeze. The choice of the native stone for the walls in combination with brick was also a nod to early builders, as were deep eaves on the western elevation to shade the house from the intense sun. Here, on this western face, Williams's hand appeared freer and his interest in simple building forms more expressive, as, for instance, in the central bay, which convincingly represents a frontier structure enveloped by the overall cleaner exterior lines of the house.

Once inside, a highly decorative space unfolds, but with Williams at the helm the ornament is intrinsic, not applied or affected. For instance, wooden beams and mantels were hand carved by Lynn Ford, brother of O'Neil Ford, who collaborated with Williams at the Drane house; iron doors were hand forged; plaster walls have the craftsman's touch; and the stone floors, once the pavement of Corsicana streets, lend their warm patina to the overall theme.

Two of the most charming spaces of the house are also the most puzzling, for they show the Texas-focused Williams reveling in his penchant for the picturesque. In the small library just off the hallway, or the spine of the house, one sees medieval Europe conjured in the Williams-designed rug of alphabet letters (based on the initial letters from one

of his illuminated manuscripts), the painting *St. Jerome in His Study* (based on an etching by Albrecht Dürer), and the scrollwork of the fireplace mantel. Outside, in the formal courtyard beneath the shadows of heavy beams, a flooring of mossy bricks gives way to a spiraling staircase leading up a small tower to a dovecote.

If the frontier seems far away in these spaces, it is because indigenous architecture concerns itself with the elements of design—capturing the breeze, understanding how to use local materials, creating a shelter in the prairie. In the days ahead, O'Neil Ford would take Williams's lessons about frontier structures into the realm of modern design. His was a different era, after all. But Williams was the pivotal player. Without his profound influence, who knows how native Texas architecture might have evolved.

LEFT: The living room mantel and ceiling beams are ornamented with the carvings of Lynn Ford, brother of architect O'Neil Ford. The floors are of stone taken from the streets of Corsicana before they were paved over.

BELOW: The courtyard looking toward the rotunda of the interior hallway. Notice the brackets holding up the eaves—the wooden beams overhead are given the same treatment, all with an eye toward creating the picturesque.

OVERLEAF, LEFT: Williams called this space the rotunda. It is about midway down the long hallway that opens the house on both sides, allowing breezes to flow freely. It also provides the opening to the courtyard.

OVERLEAF, RIGHT: The foyer with highly ornate plasterwork and graduated architectural shapes over and around doorways. The butterfly motif is personal to the Cooks, who transformed the house after years of neglect.

BELOW: The floors of the Drane-Cook house are covered with recycled stone taken from Corsicana. It is particularly noticeable in the dining room and the living room.

BOTTOM: The conservatory, with a shallow barrel vault and fountain (the painted ceiling and restored fountain vary slightly from Williams's original intentions). Williams's artful combination of stone and brick is one of the most picturesque aspects of the room.

RIGHT: Williams's masterful little study for the Dranes has been painstakingly restored by the Cooks, including the recreation of the original carpet, which illustrates the alphabet in Roman characters. It was taken from a page in one of Williams's rare books. The artist of the painting over the fireplace is believed to have been Williams's friend, Tom Stell.

THE STABLE

"The idea occurred to me, as I looked around at those lovely trees, that there might be some money in it, if one could get some of that land and cut it up into home sites." So remembered Hugh Porter of a day in the early 1920s that he spent with his buddy Mike Hogg riding horseback through the wild, undeveloped woods of Buffalo Bayou near Houston. The inception of the idea was as simple as that, but it began to grow in magnitude and reality after Mike Hogg mentioned it to his brother Will, who instantly seized upon it and doggedly acquired eleven hundred acres to be divided into lots. Will Hogg was devoted to the betterment of Houston, as was Mike and their sister Ima (see page 50). By 1924, Hugh Porter was president of a development corporation, and the suburb of River Oaks was well on its way to becoming an elite neighborhood. In fact, long before astronauts were uttering "Houston" from outer space, this neighborhood was doing the job.

The launching of River Oaks coincided perfectly with the nascent architectural practice of John Staub in Houston. He had arrived in the city in 1921 to open an office for his employer, New York architect Harrie T. Lindeberg (noted for his high-society country homes), but Staub set out on his own in 1923 when he was hired to design the River Oaks

Country Club. In the years to come, he would design dozens of homes in the neighborhood, including Ima Hogg's famous mansion Bayou Bend. Her home, which houses a major collection of American antiques, demonstrates how original he could be within the framework of a specific, eclectic style. Here, Staub melded a New Orleans aesthetic with a basic Colonial structure, creating a house that seemed peculiarly right for subtropical Houston and Miss Hogg's graciousness. Such subtlety of form and concept was not always apparent in the neighborhood. Many who had purchased sites wanted big, showy homes that filled the lot and were easily visible from the street. If they hired Staub they got a sophisticated version of almost any style—Colonial Revival, French manor, Italian villa, even Modern—filtered through his highly refined sensibility. The time was coming when it might be said that owning a house in River Oaks was one thing, but owning a house there by Staub was something else.

The experience in River Oaks acquainted the young Staub with those who had been in the oil business since the great gusher Spindletop exploded in 1901 and opened the fields of Texas to exploration. Unlike the many wildcatters who populated the city, this group had the low-key style of old money and culture. The well-educated Staub from

PREVIOUS PAGE: Doors, scaled to the size of the horses that used to live within, opened directly to a line of stables. Houston's elite loved to gather in the large rooms on either side of and perpendicular to this central gable. Second-floor windows lightened the room of the horses' groom, and the chimney at the apex of the gable roof vented his fireplace.

BELOW: The back door of the Stable at twilight seems to beckon home the (now absent) horses. An artfully placed window reveals the strict rhythm of rafters, which, though practical, are a decorative element as well.

OPPOSITE: The stalls that remain after a 1955 remodeling.

Knoxville, Tennessee, was a natural fit in their world. He was to design homes for them and their children for the better part of his career. One such dwelling became the de facto setting of private social gatherings so enjoyable as to become legendary. It was a home, a stable for horses that also accommodated people in a delightful manner free of pretense and formality, and hidden deep in the piney woods just beyond the reach of urban Houston.

The original stable commission came to him in 1930 from the owners of eighty acres of land. The wife of the couple was an avid equestrian who needed stalls for her thoroughbreds, an apartment for their trainer, a tack room, and a living room with an adjacent bedroom. Some years later (1955) she would ask Staub to alter the use of the stable by decreasing the number of stalls to create a large living room and by adding a swimming pool and a tennis court. But it was the first structure—the stable—that set the tone for what was to come.

The project came to Staub soon after an extended trip to Europe where, among other things, he had been impressed with buildings in Belgium, with their formal entrances characterized by a double-height frontal gable that abutted a long perpendicular gable. There was also a prototype among Lindeberg's early works where a central gable dramatized a stable with a clock near the apex of the roofline; Staub was to adapt the typology to his client's needs. In his hands, the central gable was opened wide with doors that were tall enough to accommodate an equestrian on horseback, who could then proceed through a foyer to the row of stalls on axis with the entrance. On the second floor, above the foyer, was the trainer's room, with a balcony overlooking the horses below. On either side of it, rooms in the fashion of medieval great halls balanced the stable core with a scale in proportion to their oversize doorways. Within these rooms, pairs of glass

doors stretch to the ground, and overhead, exposed rafters of wood taken from the derrick at Spindletop soar upward in great spiderwebs of beams and trusses.

Everywhere, one has the impression of natural materials used frankly and imaginatively. Red bricks are employed artfully to shape the quoins and arches around doorways and over windows, appearing in relief against a field of white-painted bricks. Wooden details, particularly in the front door, are simple and bold. The brick walkway to the front door stretches through the space without interruption—all the way through the stalls and out again.

No horses live in the Stable now, but something of their living, breathing physical presence remains. One need only open the front door to feel it. And the home they inspired Staub to imagine? It continues to attract family members and friends, offering respite and conviviality. The city has crowded in on it, but it's still secluded in the woods.

OPPOSITE: Before the number of stables was reduced in 1955, this second-floor balcony allowed the groom to continue to monitor his thoroughbreds even after he had retired to bed.

BELOW: The 1955 remodeling replaced all but four stables with this spacious room for family gatherings. The kitchen was also enlarged and a bar was added.

OVERLEAF: These two rooms, each on opposite sides of the brick-floored entrance, share Staub's interest in a dramatic use of wood from the famed Spindletop oil derrick. Sturdy and lofty, the rafters in these rooms seem to celebrate the mythic gusher that opened the oil fields of the state and, in its wake, shaped Houston and the Stable.

HALBREICH HOUSE

When she was a young girl, Nancy Halbreich, who shares this home with her husband, Jeremy, had an armoire in her room that seemed just as magical as the wardrobe in C.S. Lewis's *The Lion, the Witch, and the Wardrobe*. That is to say, when you opened the door, you could walk inside and, before long, find that you had moved beyond what must have been the back of the armoire into another dimension altogether—a large room, in fact. There were no friendly centaurs awaiting or cozy little cottages in the snow, but just as wondrous, perhaps, there were clothes—rows of ball gowns and party dresses, shelves of hats, and racks of white blouses, tailored suits, feather boas, and black slacks stretching into infinity. Something about this altered reality, this play on your expectations, imbued even out-of-season clothes with enchantment.

A bit of that same enchantment lies beneath the surface of the Halbreichs' residence now. The architectural rethinking of an undistinguished house by an anonymous architect, with a front-door entrance just steps away from the curb of one of Dallas's busiest streets required a certain vision on the part of the new owners. Nancy Halbreich instantly imagined what might be if the orientation were reversed

so that the back (via a drive into the property) became the entrance, and the front, now almost completely obscured by a tall fence, became the back. What had been simply a back-yard then became a sylvan landscape of mossy mortared cobblestones, white blossoms in rusty calyx kraters, stone steps offering changes in elevation, and an allée of Savannah hollies and sculpted boxwoods adding order and refinement. One moves through the garden not toward a back door but toward the glassed-paned arches of a loggia outstretched across a terrace—thus entering the house as effortlessly as Lucy slipped back into the wardrobe, the beauty of Narnia at her back.

On the interior of the house, the loggia creates a gallery space so rich with natural light that it serves to illuminate the interior core. The gallery also sets the tone for the house, which is essentially lyrical, in spite of its dignified European overtones. For instance, as one enters the vestibule at the far left of the gallery one can look laterally across space, over an outdoor pathway, and through a glass door to a separate wing of the house. There, the lines of perspective (set up by a pair of arches in the gallery) converge at a focal point in a trompe l'oeil architectural detail in the orangery, where the

PREVIOUS PAGE: Nancy Halbreich designed this orangery as a place for her orange trees to spend the winter, endowing it with a skylight and a tromp l'oeil garden setting of painted tiles drawn from books of architectural follies.

BELOW: With the creation of a loggia of glass-paned arches across the back of the house, a new formal entrance was created, and an ordinary backyard was transformed into a French-style garden.

OPPOSITE: The Halbreichs' remodeling opened all the first-floor rooms to each other, creating a flow of spaces. Here, the arches reveal the dining room and living room in succession.

OVERLEAF: The raising of the staircase gave more architectural play to the bay window, which was formerly the front door of the house.

couple's orange trees spend their winters. Halbreich conceived of the room, with its grand skylight and its blue-and-white tiles, and then set about finding the images of gardens and random architectural details in reference books devoted to follies. In the tradition of nineteenth-century culturati, her hunt was a search for the picturesque.

As one moves deeper into the house, one comes closer to the activities of living in the home—the living room, the formal dining room, library, and informal dining room. These are the spaces of the original house, likewise inverted. Where once was the front door there is now a bay window, and, though the staircase is original, the Halbreichs raised the landing to heighten the ceiling in the living room. This staircase, with its grand ironwork and hairpin turns, is the predominant architectural feature in this older section of the house, weaving together the house both horizontally and vertically. Along its landing, iron-mullioned windows of translucent glass hide the busy street beyond, while showering the living room with soft light.

These are opulent rooms, filled to the last detail with antiques and artworks bearing impressive pedigrees. They shed light on Nancy Halbreich who, with her husband, chose them to enliven this house. She tells a story about purchasing an eighteenth-century Italian Rococo desk at a Sotheby's Parke Bernet auction, which may best describe how she approached this home. The desk was covered in what appeared to be black paint (it turned out to be smoke damage) when the couple bought it. But Nancy Halbreich was convinced that there was something wonderful beneath—so convinced that when, after the sale, an anonymous call came in asking what she would take for it, she answered $1 million, not wanting to part with it. The caller demurred, declaring, "The buyer must be a Texan!" Several weeks later, a restoration artist painstakingly cleaned the darkness away,

revealing an abundance of colorful birds in flight and exotic flowers against a field of yellow ocher. There had been hints that the desk might be something more than it appeared, but it took the Halbreichs to imagine its hidden virtue and to bring it out in all its glory.

LEFT: The new entrance foyer with a Louis XVI giltwood mirror and console, and a coat of arms inlaid in mosaic on the floor.

BELOW: All the interior rooms of the original house were illuminated by the addition of the light-filled loggia. Here, a portion of the living room is pictured.

BOTTOM: The sitting room off the master bedroom, with its views of the formal garden.

BELOW: The orangery is the focal point of the perspective lines set up across the loggia.

OPPOSITE: The owner of the house, Nancy Halbreich, is an art historian who worked for Sotheby's, where she honed her knowledge of decorative arts. When she bought this Italian Rococo desk at auction, a sixth sense told her that beneath the blackness of smoke damage there might be something wonderful.

CRESPI MANSION

Beyond the ponderous pillars and iron gate, the drive meanders across twenty-eight acres of tree-filled parkland until, suddenly, around a bend and past an allée of pines, the stunning house is before you, each fine sculptural flourish and orderly quoin boldly delineated. It's not Versailles, as the local newspaper described it, and it's obviously not Daphne du Maurier's fictional Mandalay, but it is, as the author might have it, "a jewel in the hollow of a hand."

In a city that prides itself on its mansions, the Crespi Mansion is Dallas's most legendary, the locus of glamour and wealth that transcends even local standards of privilege. It hails from that moment in American residential design when the desire for romantic allusions to European architecture was at its high point. Yet here it stands defiantly. It's not merely a re-creation of a European villa; it *is* a European villa, the felicitous result of the collaboration of an Italian count, an aristocratic Swiss architect, and a Waco-born beauty for whom the adoring count named the house.

Some say that the Villa Firenze was built on the acreage of a former cotton field, which, if true, is a suggestive touchstone for Pio Crespi. He arrived in the United States in the mid-1920s, the son of an affluent Milanese family who owned three newspapers and ran cotton mills. He had come to buy American cotton to ship home, and had settled first in Atlanta, Georgia, before coming to Texas, which in 1925 was producing between 20 and 30 percent of the world's production. It was in the course of doing business in Waco that he first laid eyes on Florence Wigley and became determined to marry her.

Family members believe that the Crespis embarked on the house in 1936, and archival photos suggest that materials for the house might have begun to be stored on the site at such an early date. However, a letter of December 6, 1939, from the architect Maurice Fatio to his father in Geneva fixes the moment when the architect first met with the couple: "I have just returned from a fifteen day trip to Texas," Fatio wrote. "I had corresponded with a man from Dallas who wants to build a villa, and I decided to see him in person to assure myself of the order."

In the course of the letter, Fatio eagerly describes what he saw in Texas—cowboys at work, cotton and sugar cane plantations, and oil wells—but the client he had come to see was going to veer him away from all that, back, in a manner of speaking, toward home. What Crespi wanted from Fatio

was a European villa, inspired by one in Milan owned by his cousin. Fatio was the right choice of architect: He had built a reputation for the Italian villas he had designed (with William Treanor) in Palm Beach, but these estates, for the Vanderbilts and Schiffs among many others, were Italian villas with distinctly Mediterranean aspects, such as tiled roofs, picturesque outdoor staircases, and cloisters. The Crespi house was to be more formal and contained, more coolly elegant and refined. Its roots were northern Italian and not so unlike the Villa d'Este on Lake Como, where the Crespis kept a suite each summer to escape the Texas heat.

The plan of the first floor follows the formality of the exterior, by means of a wide marble-floored gallery that fills the house with light. The central, public rooms of the house organize themselves along this gallery, such that the circular classicism of the stairway hall, the acid green upholstery and chinoiserie of the bar, the wood paneling and warmth of the library, and even the formal living rooms are entered principally from it. The formal and informal dining rooms follow the same pattern to the right. But the gallery itself is much more than a means to an end. While it orchestrates movement through the house with the rhythm of its arches and pilasters at each bay and its repetitive chandeliers, it also provides perspectival vistas through the house and, not least, facilitates entertaining on a grand scale.

As the house has changed in style from the Crespi's lavish eighteenth-century French furnishings to the crisper, more eclectic style of the current owners, the constant has been the desire to open it up for parties and events. As Florence Crespi once told her granddaughter, "There is something about the house that delights people."

OPPOSITE: A bronze female nude grandly occupies the stairwell hall just inside the entrance to the house. From her vantage point, one can appreciate how well the front gallery illuminates the interior of the house.

BELOW: The chinoiserie of the fine chandelier and the Italian plates on the wall, each one depicting in sepia tones a different Roman monument, combine to make this breakfast room one of the most appealing in the house.

BELOW: The gallery of the Crespi house, from which every first-floor room is entered. Extremely wide and appointed with artworks and chairs, it expands the possibilities for large gatherings.

OPPOSITE: At the end of the gallery lies the living room, which has exposures to the garden on three sides. The effect is a spacious, light-filled room where the sun heightens the sculptural quality of Fatio's moldings and coffered ceiling.

OVERLEAF: The bar possesses all the sophistication of a 1930s Art Deco bar complete with acid-green upholstered chairs, silver furnishings, and mirrors painted with scenes of Chinese daily life. The room has remained unchanged since the Crespis lived here.

PARROT-ORLOWSKY HOUSE

Tulsa, Oklahoma, and Dallas may not seem like the kinds of places that would engender and nurture a taste for French-Norman houses, but in 1930s America, with the winds of the Dust Bowl just kicking up and the Great Depression in full swing, dreams of other times and other places made perfect sense. This was not the historicism of aristocratic, Beaux-Arts-trained architects who traveled the world sketching ideas to funnel into "traditional" houses for high-society patrons. No, this was eclecticism born of an imaginative leap in which a mind's-eye vision of dovecotes in gabled roofs, Juliet balconies, turrets, and Dutch doors was enough to inspire delight and the romantic architecture of this house.

Such, at least, was the case with Charles Stevens Dilbeck (1907–1990), who grew up the son of a builder in Tulsa. A precocious young designer with only two years of college, he had managed to land commissions with some of the city's oil-rich citizens. However, when the stock market crash devastated the Oklahoma economy, he headed to Dallas in the hope of finding greener pastures. And he succeeded. Almost immediately he received commissions from wealthy citizens and work with builders who were opening up new subdivisions. He also became friendly with Dave Williams and

O'Neil Ford, who were just then putting their observations of frontier structures to use.

To Dilbeck, the idea of designing a house that is in sync with its environment, particularly in terms of ventilation and use of local materials, was second nature. He shared Williams's interest in early frontier building, but his references were the ranches of the Panhandle and the plains of West Texas, not the *fachwerk* homes of the Germans and Poles. And there was another key difference. While Williams and Ford distilled the essence of the frontier house, sometimes masking it with crisper, more contemporary lines (see the Drane-Cook and Bromberg houses, pages 80 and 126), Dilbeck was drawn to the rough edges left by the pioneers, especially apparent in their additions to log houses in which they used whatever means and materials available. In this regard, the Texas ranch house and the French-Norman cottage were not so different to Dilbeck. It was the tradition of rusticity that motivated him. To come across the story-book charm of his homes ensconced in the elite, often self-consciously opulent neighborhoods of Dallas is to understand why Marie Antoinette fled Versailles for the comfort of her picturesque architect-designed retreat Le Petit Hameau de la Reine.

PREVIOUS SPREAD: One of the hundreds of houses Charles Dilbeck designed during the middle years of the twentieth century, accommodating the French Norman–style farmhouse (or frontier ranch house) to the Texas landscape. Here, the house takes shape around an oak tree, with a frontal garage posing as the house proper. In fact, the second floor, surmounted by a dovecote, is a guest bedroom.

OPPOSITE: A classic Dilbeck detail is the joining together of the garage gable with the wall and roof of the tower (with balcony), with bricks laid at angles within pegged boards (to the left and slightly above the balcony).

Dilbeck was a prolific architect. It is estimated that he produced as many as four hundred houses in Dallas alone, and many more, usually ranch houses, outside of the city. Yet, of the dozens of houses he designed during the 1930s and 1940s, this little house for Lois and Oliver Parrot stands out. Oliver Parrot was a contractor who was employed by one Frank Parrot (presumably his father) who lived near a neighborhood dominated by Dilbeck houses. Like the houses Dilbeck designed for a builder there, the Parrot house was quite small, and, like many of the others, it bore all the blandishments of the French-Norman farmhouse—though not necessarily as you would find them in Normandy.

In 1939, the Parrots presented Dilbeck with a lot endowed with a large live oak tree, which gave him the opportunity to turn a garage sideways to be entered off of a semicircular drive around the tree. On the street side, the garage displayed a steep gabled-house form, with an attic dovecote and the windows of an upstairs bedroom. At street level, the garage was punctured with small openings and latticework on the wing wall of the gable. Beneath it, a low wall of fieldstone supported a bronze rooster, cockily alerting visitors that they've entered a virtual farmyard.

Beyond the garage, the house stretches along the lot parallel to the street but with such changes in roof shape and materials that it appears much larger and complex than it actually is. A bay window and a doorway mark the point where the garage meets a small tower with a hipped roof that denotes the rise of a stairwell within. A Juliet balcony overhangs the windows of a dining room, and because it stretches out laterally beyond the tower, the gable roof of the interior's great hall is suggested. All of these forms, but for the wooden windows and doorframes, are clad in fieldstone. And yet, to the right of the red Dutch door of the main

entrance, the house becomes brick between pegged timbers. The effect is that of an addition made of found brick laid askew when no more fieldstone was to be had. There is also a bit of crooked brick connecting the tower to the roof above the bay window.

Inside, one discovers Dilbeck's great belief that a small house should be every bit as thrilling as a big house. He transforms the traditional living room into a great hall with exposed rafters that curve above one's head into arches, dramatizing the staircase adorned with quatrefoils. Appropriately, the newel post is a giant acorn. At one end of the room a fireplace of ill-shaped, picturesque clinker bricks fills the wall. Opposite, a small hallway leads into a dining room with a coffered ceiling.

By all accounts, Dilbeck loved designing houses, and something of that pleasure comes through in his body of work. There is a certain sense of fun in his refusal to use French form in a prescribed way. He kept a well-thumbed book on the subject in his library, but he took liberties, just as the indigenous Normans themselves took liberties. Like them, he simply designed according to his own informed instincts and imagination and the available resources. Is it possible that, were he living in the Middle Ages, he might have made the same design decisions as his counterparts of that time? Perhaps. When Dilbeck visited Europe for the first time after his retirement in 1961, his wife, Pat, recalls a moment when his usual light-hearted personality took a sudden turn. They were standing in a monastery in Normandy, and Dilbeck became uncharacteristically grave. "He got very serious," she recalls, "and said, 'Look, I feel like I designed this place.'" And, she says, "For a long time afterward, it haunted him."

LEFT: Dilbeck delighted in making a small house feel large with rooms such as this, the great hall, with its towering gabled ceiling of exposed rafters. He rarely used brick that was not recycled or in some other way bearing the marks of character. Here, the hearth is a picturesque combination of short and long bricks laid asunder for effect.

BELOW: Looking back at the opposite end of the great hall, the staircase (note the acorn newel post) is very much a part of the room, bringing home the medieval overtones of the house with the carved quatrefoils just below the railing.

BOTTOM: A French country–style corner fireplace in the library.

3

MODERNISM
SUITS TEXAS

The Bass house.

BROMBERG HOUSE

The hope that a beloved home won't be changed beyond recognition after it is sold is a common desire. But imagine a boy (now an adult) who grew up understanding the value of his family home not merely in terms of sentiment or economics, but in terms of historical importance, and you have a situation in which the seller is willing to wait for the right buyer—someone who will not only respect the architecture but (and here's the clincher) sign a contract agreeing not to change it without the seller's approval.

To understand such loyalty, one must flash back to the late 1930s when the architect O'Neil Ford, who would become the most influential architect in Texas, was just getting started. During the Great Depression, he had managed to receive enough commissions in Dallas to reveal his singular talent, enough, that is, to interest Mr. and Mrs. Alfred Bromberg, who wanted a modern house for themselves and their young son. In 1939, they contacted Ford, then working in partnership with Arch Swank, about the prospect of designing a house on a five-acre lot in an area of wild, undeveloped farmland on the edge of Dallas. It was a seminal moment in Ford's career: He was no longer working with Dave Williams, his mentor (see page 80); he was well under way with the now-celebrated Little-Chapel-in-the-Woods

for Texas Women's University; and he was unconsciously on the brink of a fateful move to San Antonio, where his unique talent would flourish, bringing fame in its wake.

The Brombergs were intellectuals and well acquainted with Dave Williams and the bohemian circle of artists and architects who revolved around him, particularly the young O'Neil Ford, whom Williams promoted. Although he was only a child at the time, the Brombergs' son, Alan, remembers that Dave Williams "had much to do with our interest in Neil." His mother explained why in a 1984 taped interview with historian Mary Carolyn George: "Dave always said Neil was a better architect than he was," Juanita Bromberg said, "because Neil had never gone to architecture school." Even so, Ford certainly didn't strike the posture of a successful architect. After receiving the Bromberg commission, he was continually asking them for advances on his fee to keep his telephone from being cut off or to make a payment on what Mrs. Bromberg called "his perfectly horrible, huge car." It hardly mattered; the Brombergs also found him "perfectly wonderful to work with."

Ford, like Williams before him, was irresistible. He was quick-witted, well-read, original, and so facile with ideas and the pencil that sketched them that he astonished those who

PREVIOUS PAGE: It is often difficult to recognize newness in work that is more than sixty years old, but when O'Neil Ford designed this house with its screened porches, it was clearly a modern statement. Arch Swank, one of Ford's most talented partners, collaborated with Ford on this house.

BELOW: A corner of the screened porch with a view into the library. This fireplace, with a surround of Mexican tiles, is one of six fireplaces in the house. They are masterful details in a house full of handcrafted forms.

met him. It's the oldest story in the book—the easy talent of an architect dazzling a client on a napkin or torn envelope—but each chapter and verse in this book tells a different story. For Mrs. Bromberg, this moment came when she asked Ford about a ceiling in her house, and he replied, "Oh, that's no problem," and then "[he] searched around in his pocket for a stubby pencil," she recalled, and handily sketched off the idea.

Just before the Bromberg house design got started, Mrs. Bromberg gave Ford a book on the Bauhaus architects of Germany, which can only be understood as an indication of their interest not in the Bauhaus per se, but in a simple, modern house void of the clichés of conventional suburban architecture.

The house that evolved was sited deeply back on the lot with a long drive into the property that made a full circle in front of the house. And what the visitor encountered as he or she pulled up that driveway was a house beautifully, rhythmically swathed in screen porches and in balconies where balustrades marked the same modular beat as the supports for the screens below. The true structure of the house could be found within these graceful appendages. To find it one needed only follow the standing seams of its metal gable roof, note the simple forms of its bookend chimneys and the brick of its walls—the very aspects of straightforward frontier architecture Ford had come to admire under the tutelage of Williams.

But in the Bromberg house Ford outdid the early settlers not by adding a simple horizontal porch with deep eaves or a dogtrot (although the carport bears the appearance of such a breezeway), but by making the importance of ventilation so paramount that it dominated the exterior of the house, becoming its premier design feature. The Brombergs say they lived on these porches in the days before air-conditioning.

All trappings of the frontier vanished in the interior where Ford, with the help of his brother Lynn, who carved the three downstairs mantels, showed his virtuosity with materials and their combinations. He specified first-grade hemlock for the ceilings and cabinets, and beech for the undulating stair baluster, risers, and treads. Alan Bromberg's bedroom, upstairs, was knotty pine, as was the study downstairs. Throughout the house, mitered wood, creating a herringbone pattern, occurred and recurred on ceilings, walls, and cabinets. Lynn Ford copied the gadroon design of a favorite bracelet of Mrs. Bromberg's for the living room mantel, and the ivy design of her Spode china for the dining room mantel. A kitchen of square blue tiles with ingenious below-cabinet panes of glass allowed the cook to see the arrival of guests or to watch the children playing.

This is the house as it was finished in 1939, and this is the house that we still see today because Alan Bromberg found buyers who not only valued O'Neil Ford but who had also been active in preserving other Dallas historical structures. The buyers, Gail Thoma Patterson and Dan Patterson, did request two alterations—the addition of a family room and the adjustments needed to transform an upstairs servant's room into a wing for their daughter. Bromberg acceded to both, realizing that families live differently today than they did when he was a child, but he admits, "I felt relieved when I heard they had hired Frank Welch" (see page 244).

For Welch, who is one of the most admired of Ford's successors, the job was both an honor and another chance to learn from his friend and mentor. He refreshed the house where it was showing some wear and added the family room as a gallery across the back of the house, continuing features, such as the mitered design in woodwork, found elsewhere in the house. Now that he is finished, he acknowledges, "I used to get the nerves when I went there. I wanted so much to do the right thing. I felt his presence."

BELOW: Notice the glass rectangles in the windows in the dining room, which echo the clean geometric lines of the wood paneling. O'Neil Ford's brother, Lynn, carved ivy in the mantelpiece as a reference to Mrs. Bromberg's ivy china pattern by Spode.

BOTTOM: The library in knotty pine, the material that was also used to great effect in Alan Bromberg's childhood room upstairs.

RIGHT: The living room of the house, with its ceiling of herringbone hemlock and a curving bay window looking out to the wooded site. Lynn Ford carved a gadroon pattern, influenced by one of Mrs. Bromgerg's bracelets, into the mantel of this fireplace.

BELOW: The butler's pantry is paneled entirely in hemlock laid in a herringbone pattern, a theme running throughout the house.

OPPOSITE, TOP: The simple craftsmanship of the handrail and the beauty of the balustrade, all crafted from beech wood.

OPPOSITE, BELOW: The master bedroom's sitting room, with a sliding door leading out to a terrace and a fireplace designed and executed by the art students at Texas Woman's College in Denton.

NAGEL HOUSE

The letter is dated October 10, 1941, and begins: "Dear Nagel, It was a great pleasure indeed for me to get your letter of October 3 with the photos and plans of your house. I really congratulate you because I think it is an excellent design. . . . The plan and appearance of the house are very pleasant and you must be proud to have achieved this and even own it yourself." And then, following the prediction that the house might "burst open the way towards new architecture in your district," is the closing, "Very sincerely yours, Walter Gropius."

Chester Nagel's fine, diminutive house did not inspire a following of similarly modern buildings in Texas. In fact, it survives today as one of the few—certainly the first—truly great International Style houses in the state. Yet there was no mistaking that a bursting open of the way toward new architecture had occurred. And it had happened in the sensibility of Chester Nagel.

Born in the little town of Fredericksburg, Texas, in 1911 and instructed in the classical Beaux-Arts style at the University of Texas in Austin, Nagel arrived at Harvard's Graduate School of Design (GSD) in 1939, just two years after the school had lured Walter Gropius from London, whence

he had fled as a refugee from Nazi Germany. Gropius, the creator of the Bauhaus movement and designer of thrilling buildings of steel and glass that were completely nonreferential, was also an inspired professor and idealist. Contact with him in his role as teacher and mentor left the youthful Nagel changed for life. After school, Nagel returned to Austin long enough to design this house (for which he had a lifelong affection), and, with his friend Dan Driscoll, the innovative, sybaritic Barton Springs Bath House. By 1946 he was back at Harvard—this time as a teacher in the GSD and assistant to Walter Gropius. By 1951, he was one of the team players in Gropius's famous Cambridge firm, the Architects Collaborative.

The house Gropius saw in the photographs Nagel sent him obeyed principles the former Bauhaus director valued—that is, a systematic use of standardized materials; the manipulation of inexpensive, local materials; and a design that responded to the site and the practical needs of the house in a logical way. He would have seen, for instance, Nagel's standardized windows installed like ribbons across the south and north faces of the house; the creative use of limestone, so plentiful in central Texas; and a footprint on

PREVIOUS SPREAD: Beneath the square roofline fascia, the limestone facade of the Nagel house gently curves in an elegant concave form. Except for the living room denoted by the fireplace and wooden wall, all other rooms line up behind the curve of this limestone wall.

OPPOSITE: The eastern elevation of the house. The third level, with a precocious use of a chain-link fence for a railing, is where the master bedroom and guest bedroom are located. Access to nature was just across the plank and down the spiral staircase. The second level is the sunroom, which was originally screened and is now glass.

the property that projected the house into the site perpendicular to the street, to benefit from the natural properties of the landscape and of the climate. The house also reflected two other trademarks of the new Modernism, as practiced by the Bauhaus—white-painted surfaces and strict exclusion of all historical or conventional references, qualities that would minimize the dwelling's mass and put in relief the refinement and precision of the structural steel. In Nagel's house—indeed, in Gropius's own house in Lincoln, Massachusetts, built only two years earlier—there was a real quest for beauty (a word Nagel was not hesitant to use) born of what was appropriate for the place and the time.

Appropriate and *beautiful* are relative terms, however, and in the minds of Austin's lending institutions, Nagel's house plans qualified in neither category. Only when a local lumberyard provided backing, out of respect for Nagel's contractor, who was excited about the project, did the house become a reality. It would cost Nagel $6,600.

Nagel's lot on a secluded street in Austin was characterized by a sloping hillside that gave way to a wooded ravine at its base. Instead of placing his house along the ridge of the hillside, which was in keeping with the neighboring homes, Nagel capitalized on the topography by stretching his house across the grain of the slope, allowing the ground to fall out beneath it as it moved from the grade-level front door across a living room and beyond to a sunroom, hovering a full floor above the eastern backyard of the house. Such an arrangement, made possible by Nagel's express use of steel, provided for a view across the shady ravine and beyond to the University of Texas tower in the distance. The room, with floor-to-ceiling glass (originally screens) on three sides, bathed the interior in eastern light.

This sunroom is the culmination of the slender central core of the house and is on axis with the dramatic concave limestone wall of the street-facing carport that hides it (and the vehicles it shelters) from passersby. From the balcony formed by the sunroom's roof, the master bedroom above enjoys a view and, by virtue of a plank leading out to a free-standing spiral staircase, a connection to the ground-floor patio. A significant break from this slender core occurs on the first floor, where Nagel has doubled the space to accommodate a living room with a limestone fireplace. There, as if to show the versatility of limestone, he encourages the stone wall of the fireplace to stretch out from the ground-level hearth to become a floor. This section of the floor acts as a kind of subliminal reference to the exterior patio, as if the house was partially built on a pre-existing limestone base.

Nothing about Nagel's work could be more natural, more intuitive than his use of limestone. Having grown up in the Hill Country of Texas, a place where little more than the scrape of a boot exposes the soft white stone, Nagel could claim his knowledge of its properties as part of his birthright. In Fredericksburg, he saw it used in commercial buildings and the indigenous farmhouses and barns of the German immigrants who settled the town. He saw it during the summers working on his grandfather's farm in nearby Comfort, and he saw it in Austin when he attended college. And if this wasn't enough, he was given a college assignment (and a camera) to go back home and take photographs of Fredericksburg houses.

Maybe it is possible to say that Nagel, who was hailed as the first American architect to take the Bauhaus out to the field, away from the academy, was also, for Texans, an architect capable of showing where the distinctions between Bauhaus and regional might be blurred. In his own words, "Beauty was sought in its true and natural forms, not borrowed, not imposed. Natural laws were studied and made to act favorably."

BELOW: Silhouette of the spiral staircase proceeding past the sunroom up to the master bedroom balcony. From the interior, the sunroom seems to be cantilevered, but it is actually supported by the thin steel piers seen here.

OPPOSITE: View through the living room. Windows toward the south frame a limestone fireplace with a limestone hearth that stretches along the floor out into the room.

LEFT: A view of the dining area carved out of the open plan as well as a glimpse into the galley-style kitchen and a light-filled entrance foyer.

BELOW: The dining area with an interior wall of limestone. The beginnings of an interior spiral staircase can be seen at far left of the frame. It was added in 1983 to access the first floor or ground level of the house, which was enclosed that year.

BOTTOM: Nagel's fine sense of industrial design can be seen in the minimal elegance of this handrail. Beyond is a second bedroom, used now as a study.

142

DE MENIL HOUSE

Chances are, Philip Johnson would be pleased to see the house he designed in 1949 for John and Dominique de Menil. It is so spare that the volumes of space, the play of the sun through its rooms, and the lightness of the building's mass are as pure and clear and uncluttered as you would expect from the famed architect of the Glass House in Connecticut. Yet not long ago, this house, the first modern house to be built in Houston, was in danger of being lost forever. Dominique de Menil died in 1997, outliving John by twenty-four years, and the house—though still quite lovely when *The New York Times* covered it in 1999 on the occasion of its fiftieth anniversary—was falling apart. By 2003, a major restoration was under way, with prominent Houston architecture firm, Stern and Bucek. The family's extensive collection of artworks and furniture was removed, and the house was essentially taken apart and put back together again. When it was finished—when, that is, every detail had been attended to, from a plumbing overhaul and asbestos removal to the painstaking matching of upholstery fabrics—a skeleton crew of art and furniture was allowed to return. Now, with so few furnishings to outweigh the architecture, the de Menil house is a picture of midcentury Modernism at its most minimal and pristine.

This, however, is not the de Menil house that exists in the memories of those fortunate enough to have experienced it when the de Menils inhabited it. Be that as it may, the de Menil's modern house on its own terms played an important role in the history of Houston architecture, influencing a whole generation of younger architects and shaking up the sensibilities of the more staid members of the Houston establishment. And, according to one friend, those were precisely the reactions the de Menils hoped their new home would provoke, for they were determined to kindle an interest in contemporary art among Houstonians.

As recent immigrants to Houston from Paris in the 1940s, the couple had been surprised by the city's resistance to contemporary art, which they had begun to collect while still in France. By the time they arrived in Houston, they had become connoisseurs of modern art, frequently purchasing works of obscure artists who later became universally sought after (the Menil Collection in Houston testifies to their extraordinary insight and passion). Needless to say, they trusted their own judgment, and when they hired Johnson (after flirting with the idea of hiring his mentor, the more experienced Mies van der Rohe), they knew they were banking on an unproven architect.

The well-tailored, urbane Johnson first visited the de Menils in the conventional two-story home they occupied with their five children and saw the lot they had purchased on San Felipe, on the edge of River Oaks. "They were so poor," the elitist Johnson told the architect-writer Frank Welch in an interview. "They had this big piece of property but wanted to build the house far enough back so that the front part could be sold off." Apparently, Johnson had not yet learned that modesty and lack of pretense in no way indicated financial insecurity. As it turns out, Dominique was an heiress to the Schlumberger fortune, amassed by her father and uncle who had established an oil well and logging company. John, who was from a noble French family, was trained as a lawyer, but had gone to work for Schlumberger after their marriage. When John became head of the Texas operations for the company after the war, the family moved to Houston.

Had Philip Johnson been a native Houstonian, he would have been tipped off about his clients by their choice of lot and their desire for the house to face San Felipe, which is not only a busy street, but also the servants' access to the grand houses facing south toward Meadow Lake Lane. Not for them the class-consciousness of old-world Houston—their egalitarian spirit, in fact, precipitated generous programs and support of the city's beleaguered African-American community. Indeed, they wanted Johnson to design them a house in which even the rooms were to be guided by a kind of democratic spirit, a directive that precluded a hierarchy of spaces. And, moreover, they wanted it be functional and easily managed without the need for servants.

Johnson is hardly the architect one would think of in terms of democracy. He was in fact the antithesis both intellectually and architecturally, not to mention temperamentally,

of those modernists in this country for whom that value was deeply ingrained. His book *The International Style*, published in 1922, had not only described what he and Henry Russell Hitchcock perceived as a new modern style, prevalent in the work of Europeans, it had castigated that of Frank Lloyd Wright, for whom building for the individual was still important. To design outside of the prescriptive typology of the new style (that could be used in any place, for any circumstance or person), was to brand one's work as *retardataire*.

But the de Menils were Europeans and Johnson fit perfectly into the mold of the avant-garde they wished to champion. They enthusiastically accepted the International Style house he designed for them. Set back from the street, the wood-frame, brick-faced house presented a long wall interrupted in the center by a wide glass doorway, and on the right (much to Johnson's consternation), two small kitchen windows. The wide entranceway passed alongside an interior courtyard, a kind of glass cube filled with the subtropical vegetation that grows so happily in Houston. It led around a facing brick wall to the living room, master bedroom, and guest room to the left. To the right of the brick wall, and around to its backside, was the dining room. Beyond that, a hallway provided access to a row of bedrooms for the couple's children and connected them to the living room. The white kitchen was opposite the dining room at the front of the house. Generous use of plate glass windows opened the house to the wooded lot beyond. Dominique made only two changes: She wanted the ceiling height raised from nine feet to ten and a half, and she wanted those two kitchen windows to the right of the front door, so that whoever was washing the dishes could look outside. On this point, she would brook no resistance.

This same determination came into play when the house

was finished. The couple felt too exposed within its confines, and they found the Miesian "less is more" approach to interiors not to their taste. And so they did something wonderfully radical, but "heretical," from Johnson's perspective—they hired not an interior designer but a couturier, Charles James, to make their house more "voluptuous." He obliged them with a sensuality of color (fuchsia and chartreuse) and materials (velvet, satin, and felt) and curvaceous forms, particularly noticeable in his lip-shaped love seats. To this reworked interior, the de Menils brought their ever-expanding collection of artwork and such friends as René Magritte, Roberto Rossellini, and Nelson Mandela. All the while, Johnson's house held its own, and the de Menils never lost their appreciation and admiration of it.

BELOW: The living room, with its floor-to-ceiling windows, offers full exposure to the landscape. While the de Menils were alive, this room was literally filled to overflowing with furniture and artwork by world-renowned artists. For a visitor, it could be awe inspiring, but for the de Menils, it was merely a part of daily life.

OPPOSITE: The front entrance, paved with black tiles from Mexico, opens to the interior courtyard at right. The de Menils' interior designer, Charles James, urged them to buy furniture—such as the pieces here—in the style of John Henry Belter. James's lavish designs seemed to tease and taunt the seriousness of Johnson's International Style house, but their opposing styles created a frisson that made for a richly artistic environment.

OVERLEAF: Another view of the living room, with Belter-style chairs, a Léger on the fireplace wall, a Scarpa lamp, and Charles James's celebrated "lip" sofa. The open door at left reveals the de Menils' bar, filled with small artworks by their friends.

BELOW: The view of the yard from John de Menil's study, where Max Ernst's portrait of a young Dominique de Menil hangs (at right).

OPPOSITE: View from the living room into the lush, tropical plants growing in the courtyard. The study is glimpsed through the windows to the right. The modernist obsession with diminishing or eliminating altogether the walls that separate us from the outdoors was masterfully handled by Johnson in this house, where floor-to-ceiling exposures open rooms to nature.

152

LIPSHY HOUSE

Dallas architect Howard Meyer belonged to the second generation of American modernists, those who, like the Californian Harwell Hamilton Harris and the Houstonian Karl Kamrath, mingled the lessons of Frank Lloyd Wright with those of Europe's modern masters. Meyer tempered Wright's influence with Le Corbusier, Harris with Richard Neutra and Rudolph Schindler, and Kamrath, to some small extent, with Dutch architect Willem Dudok, before his absolute conversion to Wright in 1947. In the 1950s all three were producing some of Texas's best modern houses, all the while grappling with the harsh elements. Harris, accustomed to the temperate climate of Los Angeles, was designing inward-looking brick houses for Big Spring and Abilene and very deep eaves for Fort Worth and Dallas; Kamrath, in his never-ending quest to emulate Wright, was cantilevering his clients' living rooms into the dense shade of Houston's River Oaks and Memorial; and Howard Meyer? Well, Meyer was designing houses like this one—blending outside and inside so seamlessly and elegantly that the sun and its heat appeared almost negligible.

Knowing how to make a house livable was one thing, but having the vision (and the courage) to interpret Texas in a modern idiom was something else. These architects may have been second generation in the larger scheme of things, but in Texas, particularly the conservative Dallas, they were pioneers. In fact, Meyer single-handedly brought the modern movement to Dallas in the 1930s, and although his life and work have never been sufficiently chronicled, he is widely credited with endowing the city with two of its most beloved buildings—the high-rise apartment building 3525 Turtle Creek (where Harris lived during an interval of work in Dallas) and the award-winning Temple Emanu-El, considered to be one of the most beautiful and important synagogues in the country.

Meyer had impeccable modernist credentials. A New Yorker by birth, he had attended architecture school at Columbia, where he worked with prominent modernist William Lescaze, who was designing his entry in the landmark League of Nations design competition. Meyers graduated in 1928 and headed to Europe with his bride (a native of Waco) to meet Le Corbusier, whose book *Towards a New Architecture* he had read while still a student. He was dazzled by the man who, he said, convinced him "that the new forms had great meaning." Corbu made it possible for the

ARCHITECTURE HAS NOTHING TO DO WITH THE VARIOUS "STYLES." THE STYLES OF LOUIS IV, XV, XVI,
OR GOTHIC ARE TO ARCHITECTURE WHAT A FEATHER IS ON A WOMAN'S HEAD; IT IS SOMETIMES PRETTY,
THOUGH NOT ALWAYS, AND NEVER ANYTHING MORE. ARCHITECTURE HAS GRAVER ENDS, CAPABLE OF
THE SUBLIME.

—LE CORBUSIER, FROM *Towards a New Architecture*, 1927

Meyers to see his recently completed homes, the Villa Stein and the Villa Savoye, and these houses, along with the work of others—Walter Gropius and Mies van der Rohe in Germany and other modernists in the Netherlands and Switzerland—rounded out and confirmed his sense of being part of a movement.

Back in New York, with his modern sensibility honed, Meyer designed two houses that received widespread publicity, and he began work at the firm Thompson and Churchill, where Frank Lloyd Wright officed when he was in New York. It seemed like a charmed life for a young architect, but very soon afterward the realities of the Depression hit hard and he succumbed to his wife's advice to give Dallas a try. They arrived in Texas in 1935, and, before the decade was over, he found himself designing a red-brick Georgian house.

This was surely a low point for Meyer with his modernist zeal, but Dallas, as conservative as it was, was also diverse, and along the way his reputation grew and clients began to seek Meyer out, eager to have a house that broke the mold of the more prevalent period-style homes that dominated the landscape. The late 1930s and the entire decade of the 1940s saw one modern house after another emerge from Meyer's small office. By the 1950s, his work had impressed a man named Ben Lipshy, who had purchased a corner lot filled with trees. The house Meyer gave him would, in later years, be labeled "the finest international modernist house in Texas."

It was not "the International Style" of white stucco and steel of the Bauhaus architects and their acolytes but the warm materials and compositional elements that referred to a specific place. Le Corbusier had written, "Mass and surface are determined by the plan. The plan is the generator. So much the worse for those who lack imagination!"

Working without a net—that is, a formula of predetermined stylistic elements, Meyer traced a plan that corresponded imaginatively to his client's needs and a fresh interpretation of contemporary life. But for a master bedroom (now a study) and a kitchen, the first floor was open, and movement through it was modulated by low, exquisitely crafted cabinets; partial walls of the pinkish, beige brick of the exterior; and a staircase hovering above a pool—a sculptural element that had as much to do with the Zen-like mood of the house as it did with transporting dwellers to bedrooms above. Wide expanses of plate glass, sliding doors, and casement windows opened broadly to the softer light of the south and north. The glass cubes of the second floor emerged from a wide redwood fascia that united and organized the disparate forms of the whole.

The great irony of Modernism is that it purported to be architecture devoid of style when, of course, its very earnest quest for purity of form and the plans that made life within more serene constituted a specific stylistic message. And as a style, it could suffer the ignominy of going out of style. And so it was that Dallas reasserted itself, and like a jungle waiting to reclaim an encroaching civilization, it overcame the Lipshy house and formalized it. The interior brick was painted white, the birch cabinets removed, the modern furniture replaced with Louis XIV chairs, and Meyer's soft, hidden lighting augmented with crystal chandeliers.

But the circle eventually came round again and two subsequent owners have brought back its original beauty. The first couple, Jim and Carolyn Clark, engaged Meyer himself in 1982. Although he was in his eighties then, he painstakingly re-created the birch cabinets, the pool at the base of the staircase (that had been covered over); pulled the original, trusted metalsmith out of retirement to restore the steel casement windows; and painted the interior brick a color

PREVIOUS SPREAD: While architect Howard Meyer rarely allowed his admiration for Frank Lloyd Wright to have too great an influence over his own designs, the Lipshy house is an exception. The horizontality of Wright's Prairie Style houses is clearly at work here.

BELOW: The large sliding-glass doors stretching across the back of the house appear more like sliding-glass walls, blurring the lines between inside and out.

OVERLEAF: In the context of Meyer's open plan, this staircase is a focal point. Hovering above a serene pool of water, its seeming weightlessness is enhanced by the steel rods that descend from above and penetrate each step.

that approximated the original natural color. Then in 2001, Temple and Mickey Ashmore worked with the Dallas firm of Bodron and Fruit to take the restoration further, essentially gutting the house, only to rebuild it (using the original plans) as faithfully as possible. Now in its pristine state, Meyer's Lipshy house takes its place among the best period houses in the state, illustrating Le Corbusier's point that architecture is "capable of the sublime."

BELOW: The sound of water in Meyer's fountain is as minimal and Zen-like as the rest of the house. From this perspective, one has a prospect of the dining room and back patio.

OPPOSITE: These built-in birch cabinets, which seem to hover just above the floor, eliminate the need for doors and walls, or any other bulky barricades.

DURST-GEE HOUSE

"Don't even ask," Larry Grantham called back to Julia Gee when she noticed him and other architects carrying woks to the rooftop of her house. It was 1978, and Gee had asked Bruce Goff to remodel and add on to the house he had built for the Durst family in 1958. As it happens, the woks (with handles sawed off) were to be used as vent coverings in this house of circles, but there's every reason to believe Gee wouldn't have asked anyway. She was the third of three owners who evinced unquestioning admiration for the architect's ideas. It was as if they all knew that Goff at his best could cast a magical spell over a place, which could easily break if adulterated by conventional ideas. As a result, this house survives today as a testament to Goff's great idiosyncratic design sensibility, each addition or alteration over the years an integral part of some overarching vision.

Compared to Goff's other iconic residences—the spectacular spiraling Bavinger house in Oklahoma and the Fords' circular house in Illinois, which were besieged by constant streams of passersby—the original Durst home must have seemed relatively low-key, going up as it did without fanfare on a cul-de-sac in the piney woods of Houston's Memorial subdivision. The scale was in keeping with the houses around it, and the brick and cedar shingles were at home in the neighborhood. Only one difference was immediately apparent. The three front windows were not rectangular or square—they were circular and they were gigantic. Goff's apprentice, Larry Grantham, and his architect friend Jim Veal, who was also helping construct the house, liked to call the windows "eyeballs," and indeed they were ocular; even the lidlike brickwork below them fosters the idea. Goff told Mrs. Gee that he liked them from the inside because you could see the whole tree through them and not just the trunk.

The windows were one way of connecting the house to the site, but Goff had another, far more subtle and interesting response to the placement of the house on the street. He sought a duet between the house and the circular form of the otherwise nondescript cul-de-sac. To accomplish this he laid the plan out in radians such that if lines were projected out from the north and south walls of the house, they would intersect the center of the cul-de-sac. Like the *sacra conversazione* of Italian Renaissance painting, in which all perspective lines converge on the figure of the Christ child, so Goff, it would seem, pointed the way to the theme of his Houston house—the circle.

On the interior, this geometry appears more subliminally,

PREVIOUS PAGE: The circle theme chosen by Goff may have derived from the nearby cul-de-sac, as one of the young architects who helped build this house recalls, but the circle was already an old friend of Goff's when he received this commission, his first from the Durst family, in 1958. Peering through the window here, one sees the circular dining table, fireplace surround, and interior "windows"—like portals—opening the bedrooms to the heart of the house.

BELOW: Mrs. Gee, who had three young children, originally hired Goff to design a playroom in 1978. This room, so like a chapel, has become an ethereal extension into the piney forest.

OVERLEAF: When Goff told Julia Gee, "Now the statement has been made," he surely had in mind this elevation of the house. Before she hired him, the house ended where the spiral staircase is now, glimpsed here through the side entrance. Her need for a carport and playroom, to the right, gave him the opportunity to achieve this perfect seesaw effect in the roofline with the cylindrical glass enclosure as the pivot point. Characteristically unorthodox, Goff covered the roofs with foam.

but there's no mistaking that the circle is the focal point. The original Durst house was endowed with a great circular dining room of glass, and a fireplace surround echoed the oculi of the front exterior. Two bedrooms above the dining room receive southern light from openings that also echo the three exterior windows. To the bedroom addition of the Starks's, the second family to own the house, Goff added a semicircular balcony matching the redwood shingles of the earlier house.

But it was in the Gee commission of 1978 that Goff's decorative sensibility and the house's form most perfectly coalesced. Mrs. Gee initially contacted Goff about adding a playroom for her three children, a carport, and a storage space, but in the end she would receive much more. When Goff came to talk to the family for the first time he asked Mrs. Gee what she liked, and she replied, "I don't know what I like." He said, "If you don't mind, I'll stay here and watch." And so he stayed with the Gees for three weeks, observing how they, but particularly Mrs. Gee, used the house. Like a true organic architect he wanted the house to take shape around the patterns of her way of life.

After Goff designed the addition, his apprentice Larry Grantham, who prepared the working drawings, began to search for a good builder. Finally, after thirty contractors refused to even bid on it, Grantham quit his office job and began to build the house himself, along with his buddy Veal and a walk-on named Dave "Fast Eddy" Cummings. They lived on the job site and developed a relationship with the Gees that was mutually warm and, Veal says, "enriching." And it was also animated by the constant stream of Japanese and European architects eager to see what Goff was up to.

Goff lengthened the galley-style kitchen enough to accommodate a little semicircular table he had designed. Beyond it a spiral staircase enveloped in glass leads up to the playroom. Another staircase on the other side of the playroom spirals down to the Goff-designed swimming pool. The playroom is a stunning room of glass from which to take in the wooded landscape beyond, with a roof overhead that slopes dramatically upward, echoing the forward lift of the roof over the Stark bedroom and balcony addition.

The Gees' desire for a carport and a storeroom ended up as a godsend for the architect, allowing him to bring the line of the roof over the Stark edition downward in a seamless descent. With these requirements satisfied, Goff turned to the decorative aspects of the house. He designed a fountain for the living room (now used as a planter) and a tile pattern to surround it and the hearth on the floor before the fireplace. The pattern of terra-cotta circular tiles, pennies, and blue circles was inlaid in green cement. (Goff watched Grantham lay these and advised him to turn some pennies over so it would be known that a human hand had laid them). The architect designed semicircular banquettes to fit beneath the bedroom eyes of the three circular windows, a half-circle love seat with a curving coffee table that completes it, and a round dining table of rebar with billiard balls supporting a glass top. This same design, without the glass, surmounts the chimney outside. The final touch was flex-glass mirrors to line the "lids" of the windows, parts of the fountain, the support piers in the playroom, and a striking door of three lowercase g's, a reference to Gee's daughter, GiGi. Goff told Mrs. Gee that the flex-glass mirrors were necessary, for without them the house was like a lady with no jewelry.

The world-renowned Oklahoma architect spent his final years practicing in Tyler, Texas, where he died in 1982. Mrs. Gee's favorite memory is his return to the house not long before his death. He walked through it, took it in, and then softly said, "Now the statement has been made."

BELOW: The eyes of a Cyclopean tribe gaze out unblinking onto the verdant landscape. At night, the flex-glass mirrors that line the interior of these windows cause them to glow and, well, twinkle.

OPPOSITE: As the young architects Larry Grantham and Jim Veal were building the house, they slept on the property beneath the overhang of the bedroom in the center of the photograph. Before the project began, Grantham approached some thirty Houston contractors, and when no one bid on the job, he left Goff's office to build it himself. This level of passionate devotion was not uncommon among Goff's apprentices.

LEFT: A short, single-run staircase ascends to the bedrooms, and from the living room one floats a few steps down to the dining room, which is ground level and closer to nature. In the foreground, one of Goff's favorite furniture devices—a long banquette.

BELOW: Beams and clerestory windows follow the roof upward. In the center of the room Goff designed a fountain, now used as a planter. The pole with the semicircular light fixture is a vestige of a partition that separated the living room into two spaces. Goff designed semicircular sofas to complement the windows.

BOTTOM: The skylight in this first-floor master bedroom demonstrates how Goff lined the interiors of his circular windows with flex-glass mirrors to achieve a twinkling, glittering effect.

BELOW: Goff decorated the door to the upstairs bathroom with a multicolored flex-glass design, which looks much like a stained-glass window. He told the Gees' daughter, GiGi, that it was a reference to her three "G" initials.

OPPOSITE: The entrance to the house is around the corner from the glass cabinet (at right), and the galley-style kitchen is through the open doorway. Goff told Mrs. Gee that he had had a hard time finding a bricklayer who would lay the brick exactly the way he wanted when the first installment for the Durst family was under construction.

WILSON HOUSE

When Jimmy Tittle was in his senior year at Texas A&M University with one year left to finish the architecture program, the school took his class on an extraordinary trip. First to Chicago to meet Mies van der Rohe; then on to Cranbrook to meet Eero Saarinen; then east to meet Philip Johnson at his Glass House in Connecticut; and finally to Lincoln, Massachusetts, where Walter Gropius was their host. Tittle and his classmates were at an impressionable age, and the exposure to these various masters of the modern movement was destined to affect their fledgling sensibilities. When school was out the following year, one of his best friends went to work for van der Rohe, while others headed to Dallas or Houston. As for Tittle, he couldn't wait to get back to Abilene. Never mind the flat landscape, the red dirt, the scarcity of trees, the curious taste for Cape Cod houses—Abilene was his element.

"I was born and raised in Abilene and we [referring to his partner, John Luther] thought we could do good work here. Then we wouldn't have to travel all over the place." And so he and Luther started their firm, the Tittle Luther Partnership, in 1958, and over the years they managed to stay put and stay busy improving their beloved little city. Even so,

an occasional house in the environs of Abilene pulled them away from home, and one of the most striking of these took shape in Eastland, sixty miles to the east.

Although the distance was not great, the terrain of Eastland bore the trademark topography—rolling hills with scrub oaks and mesquite—of the Cross Timbers District of Texas, the name given to the swath of timberland that cuts through the northern and central plains of the state. In fact, Tom and Nettie Wilson had bought a piece of land with a hill that was destined to play a pivotal role in the development of their house. They planned to build on this hill facing east, even though the span of their property presented the possibility of building on the downside of the land facing another street. While they put their ideas together about the new house, they built a small dwelling against the hill facing west. By the time they contacted Tittle, they had decided that this was where they wanted to stay.

This decision regarding the site of the new structure was critical and problematic because building against the hill, Tittle now recalls, really meant digging into it ten feet, with the result that the end wall of the living room and the master bedroom were well below the grade of the land. Beyond

PREVIOUS SPREAD: In America, the best modernists, like the architect of this house, replaced the notion of a front porch with something better—a shady walkway or patio that sometimes stretched alongside a wing of the structure and transitioned into the mood of the house before the front door was opened. Although the Wilsons asked Tittle to enclose this one in glass, it serves the same role—smoothing the abrupt transition from the outside into the interior.

OPPOSITE: The structural complexities of this house are completely lost in the graceful beauty of this sideyard and the terrace of Saltillo tiles, where the Wilsons have hosted wedding receptions and parties.

these rooms, on the exterior of the house, reinforcement walls were needed to hold back the hill.

Facing the house to the west also determined the shape the house would take. The harshness of western light precluded the possibility of a broad, open exposure to the street. Light would have to be tamed and subdued, allowed in through skylights and expanses of glass on the southern and northern elevations of the house.

Beyond these considerations, the Wilsons told Tittle that they wanted the main room or living room "to be usable at all times, not just on special occasions." They also wanted an upstairs playroom with a kitchen that could be a family game room or an entertainment space for their teenage daughters. "We were in accord with a 'form follows function' plan," says Nettie Wilson, "using Southwest materials."

To see how Tittle responded to the particular desires of the Wilsons is to be grateful that he was never lured into a practice that would have compromised his originality. His forms were bold. For instance, one large gable roof rises up over the upstairs playroom and begins its descent over the living room. In the split-level playroom, which opens to the top of the hillside, the gable creates a rising single-height ceiling, whereas the below-grade living room receives its half of the gable as a great soaring volume of space. A massive fireplace runs up the wall to the apex of the roof and beyond, while opposite a wall of windows lets in an abundance of northern light.

The stone of the fireplace is the same material that, in combination with cedar board and batten, clads the exterior of the house. It is known as Fort Phantom stone, for the short-lived cavalry post near Abilene, where Tittle says it can be easily scraped from the ground. It is particularly striking on the western exposure of the Wilsons' house, where it stands up to the sun. Laid on end with an occasional horizontal piece, it creates an effect that is less forbidding than sculptural. Around the corner to the south, it reoccurs on reinforcement walls, on the double-height columns of a terrace, and on the back wall of a garage, which together create the appearance of a private sunken garden.

Tittle would not open the house to the harsh light of the west—but he did something better. He framed a bit of nature on the interior of the house along the southern edge of an entrance corridor. Along the patio entrance of Saltillo tile (the material that covers all but the bedroom floors), one passes Tom Wilson's study, a breakfast room, and a kitchen. This cool, sylvan space was once open-air, but with Tittle's guidance the Wilsons enclosed it in glass to claim some of its natural beauty for an additional living area.

As Tittle and Luther celebrate their fifty years of practice in Abilene, they can look at a community in which their artistic contributions are apparent everywhere—colleges, office buildings, the airport, the zoo, and scores of houses. They have rarely entered their work in the annual design competition sponsored by the Texas Society of Architects (TSA), claiming they are just too busy to fill out the application. Still, word of their skill has leaked out. In 2005, Jimmy Tittle won the Kemper Award, one of the highest honors bestowed by the American Institute of Architects. When the announcement was made, a TSA spokesman said, "Through his gifts and service, Jimmy Tittle has helped everyone see the world in different—always better and more beautiful— ways. This is an achievement all the more noteworthy given that he hails from Abilene, a small geographically remote west Texas city."

BELOW: The west-facing front facade of the Wilson house. The Fort Phantom stone of the exterior is indigenous to Abilene, where a tractor can simply scrape it off the ground near the site of a deserted nineteenth-century cavalry post by that name. The board and batten is cedar.

BOTTOM: The fireplace in the upstairs playroom is copper surrounded by Fort Phantom stone. The door to the left of the fireplace opens directly to the outside onto the eastern side of the hill.

RIGHT: The staggering height and breadth of the Fort Phantom stone fireplace emphasizes the enormous scale of the living room. Tittle installed cedar lath in panels on either side of the fireplace: Oil-stained cedar was coated with wet cement that was then wiped off before it was mounted against black-painted walls. Nettie Wilson's music area to the left of the chimney has the same lath ceiling. When Tom Wilson's library of Civil War books became too large for his office, the ceiling height easily accommodated a Tittle-designed library loft (upper left).

176

BASS HOUSE

Only a year before Paul Rudolph began to design this masterpiece of residential design, his controversial Art and Architecture building at Yale University (built in 1963) suffered a disastrous fire, followed by an even more debilitating renovation. It was 1969, a year of widespread unrest on college campuses, and many believed (mistakenly) that students had set fire to it, for it had come to represent institutional rigidity and authoritarianism at its worst. Mildly put, the Brutalist concrete building had not worked. Architects were given pride of place, but painters were so cramped they could not get their large canvases into their studios, and sculptors were relegated to the basement. No one seemed to care about the great volumes of space that flowed throughout its seven floors or the areas that were light-filled or the ingenious pinwheel-like plan. Compared to its overall concrete mass, which tended to weigh down one's spirits, those lighter aspects seemed inconsequential. Who could be creative when to climb the stairs was to feel the weight of the world hanging over you?

The following year, a young couple, Anne Bass and her former husband, Sid Bass, commissioned Rudolph to design a house in Fort Worth, Texas, that would, on the surface, appear to be the antithesis of the Yale building. Whereas the Yale building was closed in and cocoonlike, with its dark brown corrugated concrete, the Bass house was to be characterized by white steel that reached out into the landscape, fostering great expanses of glass. Whereas the staircases in the Art and Architecture building were ponderous, the cantilevered staircases in the Bass house would seem to float, an impression that would be reinforced by recessed lighting beneath the treads in some of the flights.

Sid Bass was a graduate of Yale and Anne of nearby Vassar, and as students in the early 1960s they became caught up in the passionate discussion of contemporary architecture inspired by the lectures of the legendary Yale professor Vincent Scully. The Art and Architecture building was new then, and it was thrilling to the architectural community and widely celebrated. This is undoubtedly what they remembered when they contacted Rudolph, which is why the best of that building—its space, light, and pinwheel plan—came to Fort Worth repackaged on a scale and with a use that were beautifully appropriate.

For Rudolph, who was demoralized by the reversal of opinion toward the Art and Architecture building, the Bass's admiration and their conviction that he could give them the house they wanted must have offered a balm to his spirits.

PREVIOUS PAGE: In the eastern elevation, one can observe Rudolph's ingenious design, which enclosed the house while at the same time opening broad vistas of the garden. Behind the closed modular walls, Bass has expansive space for hanging artworks. The cantilevered wing to the left (not visible), parallel to the pool, is forty feet long.

BELOW: From this hillside vantage point, where a tall swing set of white steel is firmly set in the ground (just outside of the frame), the Bass house can best be understood. To the right, where the house meets the grade of the land, are service areas that recede in the context of the great outward thrusts of the house proper. Balconies dripping with ivy are suspended in midair as the land slopes gently away.

BELOW: The silhouettes of two cantilevers; each plays a role in Rudolph's overall pinwheel plan.

BOTTOM: Looking upward from the point of view of Maillol's horizontal scupture *La Riviere*, the great vertical scale can be taken in.

They were young (twenty-eight) and Anne Bass has said that their ideas were vague, but Rudolph, speaking to *House and Garden* writer Mildred Schmerz in 1991, recalled a question Bass asked that demonstrated how much she and the architect were of like minds. She asked, "Do we have to have curves, or could we just have straight lines?" As it turned out, Rudolph had already envisioned a rectilinear form.

It was not a single overall rectilinear form he had in mind, however, but numerous cantilevered rectangles, some containing rooms, others balconies, and still others reflecting the clean skeletal steel outlines of a rectilinear form. (Near the entrance, one cantilever extends forty feet beyond the house.) "The balancing of thrusting and counterthrusting spaces, often rushing through the blue, outward and upward, leads to the most dynamic of all interior spaces," wrote Rudolph in an essay for *Architecture & Urbanism* in 1977. He is not speaking of the Bass house per se, but his words articulate the precise impression one has of the house's exterior in the light of a sunny Texas day. But such busy, animated projections required discipline and balance, and one sees how subtly Rudolph controlled the forms in both the uninterrupted line of the second-floor balcony and the long section of roof that extends laterally over the courtyard at the height of the third floor. But these straight lines are hardly noticeable in the rush and drama of the projecting forms; they simply emphasize the overall horizontal aspect of the entire structure. (Graceful, gravity-defying movement brought about through a disciplined balance—could there be a more compelling architectural analogue for Anne Bass, a former ballerina whose lifelong passion for the ballet and generous support of it are famous?)

Rudolph has insisted that the thrusting and counterthrusting of the exterior are at the service of the interior, playing the critical role of creating dynamic spaces.

The notion of the pinwheel design is clearly detectable in Rudolph's bird's-eye rendering of the house, where individual rooflines are seen overlapping at ninety-degree angles, and corners of the house seem to project more than the intervening recessed rooms and courtyards. On the interior the pinwheel is more subtle, and one has the sense that it's not air that activates circulation, it's Rudolph's creation of multiple spatial volumes and the manipulation of natural light: Within the basic four floors of the house there are twelve levels and fourteen different ceiling heights.

The plan winds its way upward from a quiet beginning among beds of white flowers. Once inside, the foyer offers a view to a reflecting pool bearing Ellsworth Kelly's *Blue Disk* and proffers access to the upstairs public rooms via a staircase of cantilevered steps. A turn to the right leads to a private guest bedroom and a playroom that opens widely to the first-floor porch. At the top of the stairs one passes a grand piano and ascends a short flight of stairs to the expansive living room, where Anne Bass's artworks—by Morris Louis, Frank Stella, and Andy Warhol, among others—are illuminated with natural light; the views to her extraordinary garden, the result of her collaboration with Robert Zion and Russell Page, are especially dramatic.

The unfolding of the house continues up another small staircase to the formal dining room, private kitchen, and breakfast room. Another staircase spirals upward, past Joe Goode's *Torn Cloud* painting and Henri Matisse's *Jazz*, to the private family bedrooms.

Except for these rooms and an upstairs office, all the rooms are visually open to one another—not just across a floor but across all levels, obliterating the conventional notion of walls and ceilings. For instance, what Anne Bass calls the piano room is that space discrete from the living rooms only by virtue of a staircase of three steps; neither the

Steinway nor its music is shut off from the rest of the house, even though it possesses a sense of its own realm. Likewise, the living room offers a glimpse down to the playroom, making possible views of artworks from surprising angles and heights. Within the living room itself, a recessed sitting area seems to create a separate space for quiet conversation or reverie. Throughout, one is aware of Rudolph's skill at coaxing architectural space out of light and of Anne Bass's skill at animating the quiet of his white-enameled aluminum walls with her very personal collection of artworks.

It's been more than three decades since this house was built. It appears here now at the precise moment when Rudolph's career is being reassessed and even the virtues of the Art and Architecture building are being reconsidered and extolled. The pristine Bass house, at once classic and revolutionary, surely reestablishes Rudolph as one of America's greatest architects.

LEFT AND BELOW: Two views of the Bass dining room. At the heart of the Bass house, the shimmering dining room carves out a space with a double-height exposure to the balcony, the sweeping garden beyond (at left), and a closer, more intimate garden (below). Andy Warhol's *Bass Family Portrait* is appropriately installed above the place of family gatherings, and two Theodore Singer paintings frame the table of cut, mirrored glass.

BOTTOM: The view Anne Bass sees when she looks up from her art books. This private office, adjacent to her living quarters, is filled with family photos and mementos and is warmed on cold days by a fireplace.

4

THE FRONTIER OF TODAY

The Stretto house.

190

STRETTO HOUSE

I n 2002, New York architect Steven Holl published the book *Written in Water*. Appropriately enough, the book is filled with the architect's watercolors that capture the first whiff of an idea for a building. The title itself is classic Holl, for he is an architect for whom words have a generative power, inspiring poetic architectural form. With houses responding to Melville's *Moby Dick* and Homer's *Odyssey*, it's hard to imagine that "written in water" didn't have an equally literary provenance. Like, for instance, the heartbreaking epithet twenty-five-year-old John Keats famously dictated for his Roman tombstone: "Here lies one whose name was writ in water." The irony is that Keats had every reason to fear obscurity, whereas Holl's prodigious talent is writ large not in words (or water!) but in increasingly monumental buildings that will utter and confirm his name well into the future.

With the completion of his jewel-like masterpiece, the Nelson-Atkins Museum of Art in Kansas City, and with three buildings under construction in China (necessitating the opening of an office in Beijing), Holl has never seemed more at the top of his game. But in 1987, when the house on the following pages was first being discussed, his career was not so white-hot. He was busy, to be sure. It took him four

months to visit the Dallas clients because he was absorbed in the design of a new American Memorial Library in Berlin. But when the wall came down in 1989, the project was canceled and Holl found himself spending more time in Dallas, thinking about what would become his first freestanding work of architecture.

The clients had bought a lot near Turtle Creek, the little stream that flows through the city's greenest, most inviting residential neighborhood, but when Holl saw it, he was troubled. Oddly enough he didn't think the clients could do what they wanted to do, namely, build a townhouse on the site. So they found another place, also with a water element, and the architect was satisfied. He then took their notion of a townhouse, turned it on its side, and let the spaces flow latterly along the margin of the creek, reflecting back in architecture what he saw in the water.

But it didn't happen as easily as this suggests. One of the clients says, "Steven is philosophical. The idea gets him going." As it happened, inherent in the second site was the germ of an idea. The stream here had three small dams, which created three small ponds and the sound of water overlapping. After discussing it with a former student who is a musician, Holl decided, in his words, "to explore the

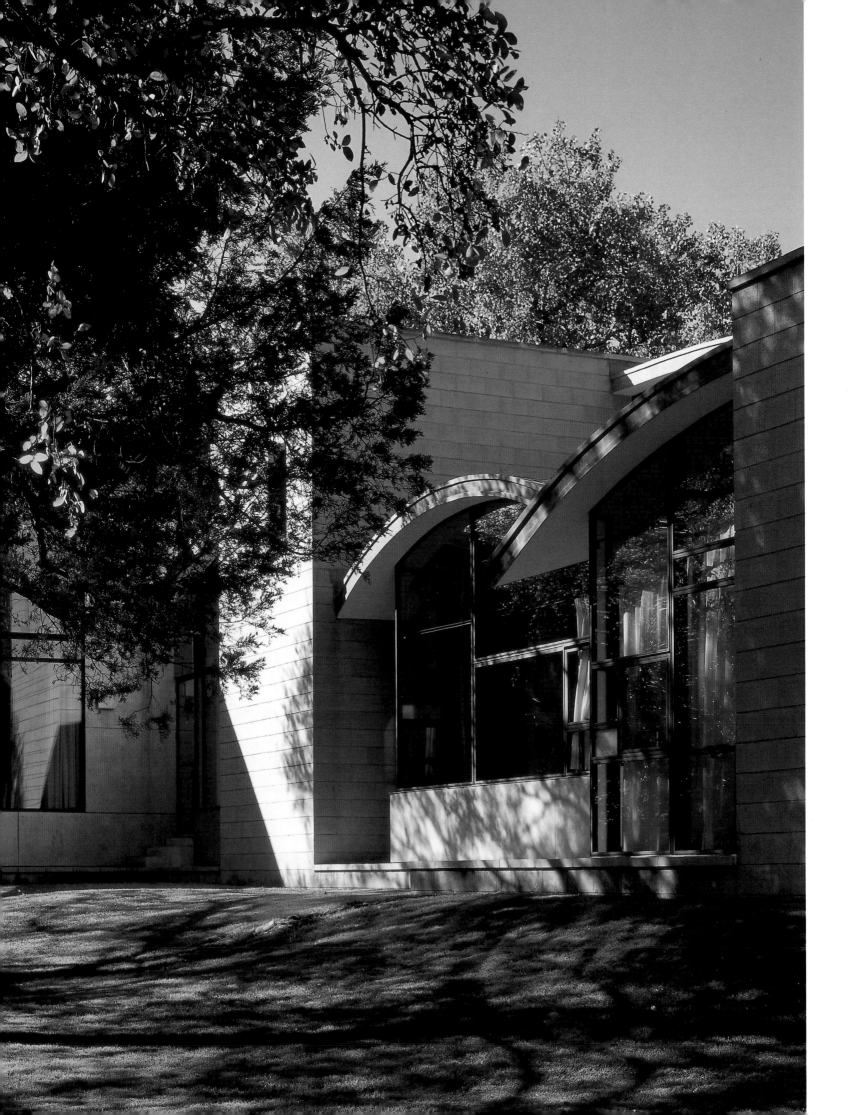

PREVIOUS SPREAD: When Holl turned the house his clients requested on its side, mimicking the flow of a small stream down the hill, he set in motion the glass and metal walls that intervene between damlike structures of concrete block. These lighter forms overlap the masonry in the form of curving metal roofs. In the window panes of the living room shown here, it is obvious that Holl was influenced by the proportions of the golden mean. References to it are clear in the window panes but can be observed elsewhere in the house.

OPPOSITE: The arc of the roofline springs from the side of an orthogonal section of concrete block and intersects with another, sending, as it were, a ripple downstream. After Holl decided that the roofs should be no thicker than seven inches, the steel pipes in the armature were bent by computer-driven magnetic induction, with special measures taken to prevent the longest pipes from exceeding the desired width.

music of stretto, which is analogous to the site's overlapping ponds. In a fugue stretto, the imitation of the subject in close succession is answered before it is completed. The dovetailing musical concept could, I imagined, be an idea for a fluid connection of architectural spaces." But for Holl this lovely stretto analogy wasn't quite enough to flesh out the concept of the house form. Béla Bartók's composition *Music for Strings, Percussion, and Celeste*, with its use of the stretto, was brought in to complete the development of the idea. Parallels were noted: Percussion in the score corresponded with heaviness of form; strings with the lightness of form; materiality in instrumentation and sound corresponded to light and space in architecture; and so on, until one realizes that there is hardly anything in the architecture that doesn't have a counterpart in Bartók's score.

The creative process is mysterious and sacrosanct, and Holl's search for analogues in the imaginative works of other artists has the felicitous advantage of widening our knowledge. But sometimes it veils and dominates his own work and one has the impulse to dispatch the intermediary and have Holl to oneself, the Holl who wrote, "Architecture does not so much intrude on a landscape as it serves to explain it."

Holl instantly gleaned the hidden meanings behind the particulars of the lot. The three concrete dams support the water, but not so much that it can't tumble into the next pond and over the following dam into the following pond. The dammed water moves forward, gradually compelled by the pond up ahead. It's that same sense of attraction, the same fluidity that draws people through the Stretto house and allows spaces to flow into and overlap one another.

Here's how he let the house "explain" the landscape: For each of the three concrete dams, Holl designed a concrete-block orthogonal space on axis with it on the hillside above.

Where there was no dam, he built a footbridge over to a guesthouse, which necessitated another orthogonal form up the hill. Then these hillside dams, parallel but unevenly placed, were bound together by the amorphous glass and metal walls on the eastern side of the house and by the floors that travel through them. One can look straight through the house—from the front door to the back, but the openings of Holl's "dams" are not perfectly aligned, and, like the water in the dams below, one feels oneself moving fluidly through the space, spilling downward, for instance, into the sunken living room or hurrying along when a space narrows, always seeking lower ground and the final connection with the stream, where, beyond his outdoor "flood room," Holl has placed his fourth dam. The drama of the house, just like the drama of the creek, is expressed in the act of overlapping. The water that flows over these dams does so unevenly and capriciously. It doesn't rush, it doesn't cascade; it just falls over itself in an arc on its way to the water below. And, likewise, the curvilinear pieces of Holl's metal roof arc over themselves, but artfully, expressionistically. One sees them leaping, as Emily Dickinson would have it, "plashless as they swim," down toward the bend in the creek, to the final hillside dam whence Holl has led our attention.

Much has been made of Holl's use of indigenous Texas materials, though, clearly, concrete block and magnetically bent steel roofs are not indigenous to Texas. The point is that the lovely Stretto house doesn't need a regionalist tag to make it important to Texas any more than Bartók needed a Hungarian tag to make his music likewise universal and timeless. Site-specific means nothing to Holl unless his architecture can somehow also rise above its place. In this sense, perhaps Holl's romantic quest for analogies is only this—a search for the secrets of transcendence.

BELOW: Ceilings within the house follow the rise and fall of the "waves" denoted on the outside, so the homeowners feel the fluidity of the house throughout. Some of Holl's furniture designs can be seen in this room, such as the side tables. The turquoise chair at far left was designed by Frank Lloyd Wright.

OPPOSITE, TOP: Passage to a staircase leading to an art library. The dark purple-blue of this small room containing the owner's sound equipment is beautifully offset by the acid gold of the pillows, as well as the screening over a stereo speaker.

OPPOSITE, BELOW: The owners are not only serious collectors of art but scholars as well, and Holl's house complements and highlights the individual works of their eclectic holdings. In the dining room, the blue pigment of the walls has the appearance of an Italian Renaissance *fresco secco* background, befitting the works in their collection. While Holl designed several of the light fixtures in the house, this one over the dining table is by Ingo Maurer.

OPPOSITE: Holl specified that the brass in the front door be acid-reddened to suggest an organic patina. The avoidance of symmetry and the positioning of horizontal and vertical lines recall the Dutch De Stijl movement and its influence on International Style architecture.

BELOW: "I told Steven, 'I'd like to waste some space,' " one of the owners remembered, "and he did a good job." Although it is far from wasted, she was surely referring to spaces such as this, which are wide open and not necessarily task specific. Such a directive was surely a boon to Holl, for it gave full play to the fluidity of his plan.

OVERLEAF: Stucco perfectly applied to reveal the thin black lines of the lath. Holl removed this corner of the living room to provide a glimpse into the sunken space. One is drawn to it, like water to a pool, as one space flows into another.

200

KNIGHTS' GAMBIT

The *Adelsverin* (Association of German Noblemen) was organized at Biebrich-on-the-Rhine on April 20, 1842, with the goal of buying and developing land for Germans seeking freedom in the new Republic of Texas. The best known of their purchases occurred in the present-day Hill Country towns of Fredericksburg and New Braunfels, but after arriving in Galveston, many immigrants, such as Adolph Fuchs and his newfound friends, chose to settle elsewhere. When the association was disbanded in 1847, it had officially delivered 7,380 Germans to Texas soil. Of these, many were highly educated, upper-middle-class professionals—"intellectuals more comfortable with a violin bow," one resident observed, "than a plough." But farming was the only option available in the early 1840s, and they bent their shoulders to it. German immigrants would ultimately exert a profound influence on the cultural and economic life of their new home (see the future of lawyer Robert Kleberg Jr. at the King Ranch, page 68), but they would never have anticipated that their very first efforts on Texas soil—the design and construction of humble farmhouses and barns—would count as one of their contributions.

The architectural imprint of German farmers on the farmland around Cat Spring was, however, negligible and, since they built in wood, somewhat evanescent. The area got its name when a young von Roeder came upon Mexican pumas drinking at the family's spring, but within eight years, the von Roeders, the Klebergs, the Fuchs, and their circle of friends were all gone, headed for parts farther west. What remained out in the fields were tall trees (often not native to Texas) bereft of the homesteads they were intended to shade.

Trees such as these stood on the hundred-acre farm Don and Elizabeth Knight purchased in 1997, and at the closing the seller revealed that she had been born in a house on the property. No evidence of that house has ever been found, but there were the trees, two mighty sycamores and one walnut, tracing out a possible footprint. Whoever had planted them knew something the architect would soon find out.

Fortunately, the Knights found their way to Houston architect Natalye Appel, a modernist with a special sensitivity to the elements that define architecture in Texas—the need for breezes; for protection from the sun; for, if possible,

[WE] HAVE TRAVELED TO THIS LOCATION ON OUR OWN, WHICH IS A TWO-DAY JOURNEY, BY HORSEBACK, NORTHWEST OF HOUSTON. WE ARE AT THE "SPRING OF THE WILDCATS" IN THE IMMEDIATE NEIGHBORHOOD OF ALBRECT VON ROEDER, WIHELM VON ROEDER, THE ELDER VON ROEDER, ROBERT AND LOUIS KLEBERG, ENGELKING (ALL FORMER LAWYERS), HOLLIEN, AMSLER (SWISS), AMTHOR AND OTHERS. FOR ONLY $200 WE HAVE BOUGHT AN ESTABLISHED FARM OF A FEW HUNDRED ACRES.

—PROTESTANT MINISTER ADOLPH FUCHS, FROM A LETTER HOME TO GERMANY, 1846

masonry that keeps interiors cool on summer days and warm on cool days. She studied the site and found that the old trees happened to occupy the highest hill on the property and that the view from it took in all the surrounding meadows, in an uninterrupted 360-degree radius.

When the Knights told Appel that they wanted a contemporary house that responded to their farmland setting, her thoughts turned immediately to the rural German homes around Fredericksburg. The area had long been a pilgrimage spot for the architecture classes she taught at Rice University. But with their commission firmly in hand, she traveled there again with the Knights' specific request in mind.

There she saw again the simple, gabled, sturdy little houses that are built of indigenous limestone and rough-hued timber in a manner known as *fachwerk*. But it wasn't the limestone construction per se that she valued, but the warm, modeled appearance it conveyed. In any case, limestone was not in ready supply in Cat Spring, so she chose a material that knows no geographical boundaries: concrete block, mixed to resemble limestone. The same material defined the structures of Max Levy's House above the Pond (page 236) and Steven Holl's Stretto house (page 190), and like them, Appel valued its clean and contemporary lines. On the outside, however, she specified a mortar technique known as the German schmear, after the plaster applied over the construction of *fachwerk* homes.

The treatment of the concrete block was a clear homage to the early German builders, and other features such as porches with deep eaves, windows to catch the breezes and carry them through, and gingerly disposed openings on the western facade were all born of frontier common sense. But Appel's Knight house is too original to fit into any genre

comfortably. Her L-shape plan embracing two of the old trees allows for full exposure to northern light and employs the trees themselves to shade two west-facing guest rooms on the short leg of the L. On the longer stem, a porch opens widely to the dining room it borders, and the doors along its length have become the principal entrances to the house. But the drama of the house occurs at the crook of the L, in the form of a three-story tower of corrugated metal: a silver silo—the mainstay of every farm, but given pride of place here and manipulated to enliven the interior of the house.

On the exterior, you see it only as a hemisphere, and there is no suggestion that the circle will complete itself on the interior with the corrugation still in place. But Appel hasn't merely alluded to a silo; she has built one and wrapped a house around it. One sees a sliver of the corrugation on the ground level of the double-height living room, and again higher up, providing access to a bridge that crosses through the space to a master bedroom. The clean beauty of the steel is unmitigated by its indoor accommodations, except in one respect. Appel has taken its function (as a stairwell) and completely subverted its hard-edge spirit by designing an ascent that rises through an undulating sculpture of white forms. Climbing it to its third-floor summit is a little like moving through clouds to a place where the sun is even brighter—in this case, a belvedere with a dramatic 360-degree bird's-eye view of the surrounding countryside.

The landscape here hasn't changed much since the Germans first saw it, and a large part of the appeal of Appel's house for the Knights is its modesty in regard to the farm's pristine beauty. There is in it a deference to those who came before and a hope, as she says, "that more and more, clients will appreciate our particular heritage and landscape."

204

BELOW: Natalye Appel says that the book-lined bridge (visible at left) traveling across the living room space to the master bedroom was, like the silo embedded in the structure, another way to bring a bit of romance into the workings of the house.

BOTTOM: The sculptural staircase spiraling up within the silo provides a glimpse of the bridge leading to the master bedroom.

RIGHT: The heart of Knights' Gambit, where the silver silo asserts itself as the pivotal player in the house plan, connecting rooms both vertically and horizontally. Through the silo, one also has access to an office in another wing of the house.

OPPOSITE AND BELOW: Like the view farmers have enjoyed from the tops of their grain towers for generations, the owners of Knights' Gambit now have their own dizzying view. The final approach up into the silo (opposite), and the belvedere (below) with an uninterrupted 360-degree perspective of the surrounding farmland and, with a little help from a telescope, the night sky.

OVERLEAF: Appel points to two aspects of indigenous Texas architecture that played on her design sensibilities. The first, related to agrarian life and German homesteads, is immediately apparent in the silo form and the manipulation of the building materials; the second, revealed here, was the hacienda-style courtyard. The dining room, just off the courtyard, comfortably mingles a farm table with the heraldry of medieval-style tapestries and thrones.

BELOW: The western elevation, protected from the harsh rays of the sun. The kitchen is beneath the lower roof section extending from the metal wall, which is softened by a country garden of wildflowers, herbs, and antique roses.

OPPOSITE: The modeled appearance of the facade is a result of Appel's use of a limestone-based concrete to cover the concrete block of the house's structure. She achieved the same effect as that of early German builders, who smeared the timbers and stone of their *fachwerk* houses with a limestone plaster.

212

LASATER HOUSE

A bit of lore attached to the phenomenally successful collaboration of David Lake and Ted Flato reaches back to the time when they were newly minted architects who had landed jobs working for the father of modern Texas architecture—O'Neil Ford. Each believing himself to be more talented than the other, they acted like young bucks, full of attitude and competitiveness, vying for position in the firm. And then, unexpectedly, Ford put them together on projects, forcing them to work in tandem. No one will ever know if the seasoned, elder architect was being wily and humorous at their expense or simply wise. In any event, his decision was fateful for the architects, for what grew out of it was a friendship and a professional collaboration characterized by deep mutual admiration and respect.

Out on their own as partners, Flato and Lake remembered Ford's love of materials and how they came together, but his lessons emerged in their work in such subtle ways that none of it would ever be mistaken for his. The Lasater house in Fort Worth eloquently makes the point, even though the shadow of Ford fell across it in the form of a client who had grown up in South Texas in a beloved Ford house.

The clients, Mollie and Garland Lasater, presented the architects with a complex site—a hillside that dropped to the Trinity River valley below, offering a multitude of views. Building on top of the hill, in keeping with all the other homes in the neighborhood, was a possibility. But looking at nature was something different from being in it, and the architects couldn't get around the fact that the most compelling aspects of the site were down below the ridge in the river bottom, where the trees were more numerous and the picturesque naturalism of a dry creek more enticing. They seemed to have a notion early on that the house could be loosely defined by garden rooms that floated in the natural landscape, blurring the lines between the interior and the outdoors. But where and how?

As the architects made dozens of sketches and the Lasaters moved lawn chairs around the site in search of the best views, Garland Lasater had an idea: "The Japanese do this very well. We should go there." On the trip that followed, Ted Flato says they visited three or four gardens a day. He was impressed that seventeenth- and eighteenth-century Japanese monarchs were creating "a highly manipulated natural world" at the same time that Versailles was being built. At Rinshunkaku and Katsura, to name just two

PREVIOUS PAGE: The public rooms, like this pavilion, want "to float off of the ground lightly," says architect Ted Flato, "becoming a member in the landscape." Stone work also partakes of such naturalism, appearing to be in its natural state, as if unquarried. But, in fact, the quarried stone of the soft creamy walls came from Sisterdale, near San Antonio, and the horizontal line of gray stone, suggesting a deeper stratum in the earth, came from Leuters.

BELOW: The kitchen touches down on a courtyard, bringing the family-room pavilion with it for an instant before it floats out again, lured by the lushness of the lowland around the banks of the Trinity River. Very deep eaves keep it perpetually cool and shady.

of the garden pavilions visited, the impression wasn't only of the siting of structures in the landscape, it was also of the details that fostered a lightness of form. Wooden floors, ceilings, doors, windows, and deep eaves with soffits of exposed timber were all of a piece in the buildings they constructed.

Back home, Flato was now certain that the top of the hill should be dedicated to the cars. That's when he, Lake, and partner Karla Greer (another Ford alumnus) began work on a "highly manipulated natural world" of their own, one that took both owners and visitors down the hill to a series of pavilions situated in the landscape. The descent is pure Lake/Flato, which is to say that the passage is accomplished with the kind of expressionistic stonework that has become the firm's trademark. Influenced by the vernacular stone building of early German settlers to Texas, they used the stone in the simplest, most honest way, which, Flato says, brings out its beauty. A stairway of cut-stone steps is bestrewn with uncut boulders, and the walls that frame it appear mortarless and even moldering, as if they had been there for centuries. A kind of stringcourse of dark gray limestone from a different quarry runs horizontally through the creamy-ocher walls, suggesting a lower stratum in the earth and enhancing the psychological effect of dropping down through solid rock. The collaboration of landscape designer Rosa Finsley, who planted the path downward in an abundant profusion of natural vegetation, helped lend the sense of a primordial landscape reasserting itself in the face of an encroaching civilization.

The archeological overtones of the approach put in relief the exquisite refinement and fragility of the find that awaits. At the doorway, clad in lightweight copper, one can see the first pavilion, a living room, also sheathed in copper and seemingly perched on a foundation of limestone, like frontier structures. A boxy bay window extends from the structure,

and glass takes the wall on up to the eaves. But the eaves are not just extensions of the roofline, their exposed structure a continuation of rafters from above. They are, rather, like large shutters held up by steel rods. Their upright nature buoys up the structure, playing a part in the architects' desire to float the pavilions in the site. Walls of windows and doors of glass extend the boundaries of the room to the lake of grass outside.

The corridor beyond the front door may be construed as as a kind of footpath through the house. (In early plans, it is even rendered to suggest that it is outside.) From it one can turn right to enter the series of rooms culminating in the master bedroom, all of which are clad in limestone to reinforce the notion of privacy. Another right farther down the "footpath" leads into a pavilion comprised of a family room and kitchen, hovering above a forested landscape and opening to a clearing that stretches downhill along the path of a rivulet. In the middle of the footpath, the architect pushed out a space for a dining table, which becomes a pavilion by virtue of its shared space with a raked garden outside. A low wall frames a small view that somehow, magically, seems to take in the whole landscape. The footpath ends at a wide staircase that leads past the gridlike panes of a picture window (echoing the entrance door) into a final hidden pavilion containing two guest bedrooms.

Flato is grateful that the Lasaters placed so much trust in him. Maybe that trust became obvious when the lawn chairs were put away and Garland Lasater began to believe that "the concept of view is a terrible concept." By listening to Flato they went from the idea of looking toward a landscape in the distance to being a part of it. And their pavilion house, with its continual revelations, has given them, in Lasater's words, "a much deeper sense of view."

LEFT: The front door demonstrates the firm's desire to blur the lines between inside and out. Through the grid of the door, one can see straight across the interior space to the opposite end of the house. Just before that wall of windows, a flight of steps leads down to a landing and through a doorway into a hidden pavilion with two guest bedrooms.

BELOW: Dropping down into the site from street level. The stone wall in its moldering, stained condition has the allure of age and depth (it encloses the master bedroom and library).

BOTTOM: In the midst of floating pavilions, the master bedroom of limestone is rooted in its place across a courtyard from the family room. The slight tower on the right is a corner fireplace.

PREVIOUS SPREAD: Adjacent to the front door, the living room is buoyed up by eaves that work more like large shutters supported by iron rods. On the far side, it opens onto a court that is shared with the dining room pavilion. The rooms can be opened so broadly that one feels as though they are out-of-doors, making it an ideal space for entertaining.

BELOW: At the end of the central hallway, an unexpected staircase leads down to two guest rooms. In keeping with the iconography of this house, their limestone walls denote privacy.

BELOW: The family room looks out toward a rivulet, the living room over a sea of grass, but this dining room, a pavilion in its own right, bears out the influence of Japan on Flato. Inspired by the famous dry garden at Ryoan-ji, a Zen temple northwest of Kyoto, he designed a raked garden just beyond the glass of this room. The view from this intimate garden makes one feel, says Flato, "as if you own the entire landscape."

OVERLEAF: In the living room, it is easy to see that the first idea for the house was only a few steps away from a large tent. This boxy volume of space—twelve feet high with flat, wooden ceilings and flaps to cover the uppermost windows—*is* tentlike. Perhaps this room is the best illustration of what Flato means when he says that the very simple shapes of the house are like "buildings with no clothes on."

NOWLIN HOUSE

On the top shelf of Paul Lamb's office in downtown Austin, there is a model of the Nowlin house from the days when the couple simply wanted a Hill Country house. It's a little dusty and hard to reach, but if you squint you can see in it a foreshadowing of the house on the following pages. The miniature cardboard mock-up is not very old as actual years go, but so much happened after it was conceived—such a layering of events and experiences and newfound knowledge—that it seems rather like it happened in another lifetime.

When they first contacted Lamb, Bettye and Bill Nowlin had acquired a spectacular site on a cliff where the former Colorado River (now Lake Austin) makes a slow bend. They didn't want to make a big cut in the limestone landscape to accommodate the house, and they were adamant about avoiding one of the hackneyed styles—Tuscan, Mediterranean, Spanish Revival—that have staged a relentless uprising in high-end lake developments around Austin. After interviewing a handful of architects, they chose Lamb because he struck them more as an artist and, Bettye says, "He didn't seem to have a style."

In fact, there is a subtle stylistic heritage running through Lamb's blood, which has its source in the work of two Californians—the modernist Harwell Hamilton Harris, whose work was characterized by the quiet forms and Zenlike use of wood, and Bernard Maybeck, the supremely inventive spirit known for his irrepressible love of drama. When the Nowlin house demanded a bit of its own drama, it was Maybeck who, at least in spirit, steadied Lamb's hand. "Maybeck would have done it," Lamb remembers thinking. "*I'll* do it."

It started with the idea of an outdoor fireplace. The Nowlins had admired one in another Lamb commission, and so the question became where they would put one on their site. Lamb found the duality of creating a cavelike space high up intriguing, so he designed the fireplace in the side of the cliff and set a stone porch around it. This structure then became the foundation upon which to perch a living room that would hover above the site, taking in its breathtaking views. So far, the Hill Country idea was still intact. But then something unexpected happened. In an effort to minimize the massive look of the porch's corners, which had to support the room above, the architect battered them, sloping the outer sides upward so that the heft would recede at the top. Then someone—no one remembers who—said something

PREVIOUS PAGE: "We worked on the house so long we began to make up legends about it," says owner Bettye Nowlin. "Part of the legend was that the big wall and the loggia were already here." The ziggurat shape crowning the living room (seen here), with its commanding view of the bend in the lake below suggests the same found quality. While it doesn't quite look like a ruin, the rough-cut limestone seems weathered by time and the elements.

BELOW: Lamb liked the idea of building a cave into the cliffside of the site, which is how the room in this section of the house, with an outdoor fireplace, became the first design to be sketched. The roof shape was drawn from Mayan ruins observed at Palenque, Mexico. The living room and what it represents—quite literally, the room for the living—is suggested in the animated, lively carved flowers that emerge beyond the ziggurat crossing.

OVERLEAF: In the landscape just below the house are these six solid granite columns, which are test cores from a nearby quarry, Marble Falls, a major source for Texas red granite. They were arranged and perfectly aligned with the help of scientists at the McDonald Observatory to channel the light of the sunset to a specific spot on the equinox, the summer solstice, and the winter solstice—days and times venerated by the Mayans.

to the effect of "it looks so Mayan," and the genie was out of the bottle.

Not long afterward, the Nowlins told Lamb that they wanted a Mayan-style house, to which he replied that he would be happy to make references here and there. But Bill Nowlin insisted: "No, let's do it right. Let's make it a Mayan building true to the Mayans." So began a seven-year immersion, not only in Mayan architecture and its relationship to landscape, but in the concomitant religious practices and the symbolism behind the decorative details and the glyphs that communicated the poetics of a different world view. The Nowlins put together a team to travel with them and Lamb to Mayan sites, which included a stone carver, a stone mason, a Maya consultant, a guide, and members of Lamb's office (see names of team members, page 254). Yet, their goal was not to copy a Mayan temple and set it down on Texas soil. "The task," says Lamb, "was to understand and appropriately borrow the forms and the craft. Then we started to decipher their program. 'Why did they use this there?'" To help with the effort Nowlin arranged for a Mayan priest to bless the team during their stay in Guatamala.

They made three trips in all, hitting the major Mayan ruins, including Uxmal; Chichén Itzá and Tulum on the Yucatán Peninsula; Palenque, in the state of Chiapas; and Tikal in Guatamala. Once, Bill Nowlin chartered a little plane to take Lamb deeper into the interior, to the village of Yaxchilan, where there is an active Mayan temple. He wanted Lamb to see it because it was a river site, like theirs, but what was more memorable was the covered, three-dimensional maze one had to negotiate to enter the town. In a reference to the underworld so important to the Mayans, Lamb utilized such a maze beneath the pool, accessible only from the lower bridge crossing over the water.

Many of the details of the resulting house seen on these pages have clear points of reference in the Mayan sites. The distinctive roof shape of the house can be found on the stone structures in Palenque; the sculpted, stylized flowers that surround the the upper level of the exterior stone facing of the living room can be seen in Tikal and Uxmal; the slanted staircase to the top of the house alludes to the ziggurat shape on most Mayan temples; and the form of the arcade beneath the walkway to the front door can be found in sacred spaces in Palenque and elsewhere. The ball court in the swimming pool was copied from Chichén Itzá, where this very sacred Mayan game was played. To Lamb, the landscape in the Yucatán was like that of Austin—limestone with aquifers—and he found it informing the shapes of the house. "There," he says, "even the smaller buildings are like miniature mountains."

Lamb carried the Mayan idea of three levels—the arcade of the underworld; the active, electrified realm of today; and the open walkway above relating to the heavens—to the front door of the house and beyond to its three levels, but inside, the Mayan references are in the capable hands of Nowlin's team of craftspersons.

The Hill Country house idea may have been scrapped, but Lamb never forgot the landscape in which the house is situated. He has made a plan that provides access to the land from every vantage point—from the middle, public level; the upstairs master bedroom; and the first floor, with its guest bedrooms opening out to the cliff. The volumes of space are high and inspiring, such as the dining room's vaulted ceiling, or low and dark and intimate, like the library with the hidden trick door. With words that would make Maybeck smile, Lamb says, "A little fantasy always improves a space."

There are three parallel entrance corridors that cross the space from the motor court to the center of the house, each stacked directly above the other to create three levels. The three entrances refer to the importance the Maya placed on the tripartite nature of existence: those that are living, those in the underworld, and those in the heavens. BELOW: In the underworld arcade seen here, craftsmen built an exquisite structure in which big stone treads gradually cantilever out from the walls. RIGHT: The primary entrance is intended for the living and leads directly to the front door and main entrance to the house.

OPPOSITE: The exterior view of the three entrance levels to the Nowlin house. The quiet articulation of stonework on the first level symbolizes the underworld; the busy, or what Lamb calls "electrified," carving of the second level denotes the world of the living; and the top level is open to the heavens.

BELOW: The genesis of the idea to create a Mayan-themed house occurred here in "the cave," built into the cliffside, which houses the outdoor fireplace the Nowlins requested when they first began working with Lamb.

BOTTOM: The swimming pool is a reference to the ball court of a favorite Mayan spectator sport, one of which is preserved at Chichén Itzá. Mayan participants in the game, who often played to the death, endeavored to get a small ball through stone hoops, much like those seen here, without touching it with their hands or feet. A bridge over this pool leads underground to a maze designed by Lamb and influenced by the one he and Nowlin visited in Yaxchilan.

BELOW: The windowless library has no door. Instead, a wall can be activated to enter or leave the room.

OPPOSITE: The vaulted dining room with pedigreed Art Deco furnishings. Emile-Jacques Ruhlmann designed the light fixture, Jean Paul the eggshell buffet, and the frieze is a re-creation of Edgar Brandt's famed "Oasis," a 1925 iron screen. The Nowlins' front door is one of the gates, which had been lost for thirty-eight years, and which Brandt had designed for the Montreal Chamber of Commerce.

HOUSE ABOVE THE POND

I t doesn't rain much in Texas, so even the hint of it—like the sun's momentary disappearance behind a cloud—fills the spirit with anticipation and longing. The ground, yearning for it too, sends up its earthy fragrance like a mating call. When it happens, the sky blackens, the thunder claps in heart-reverberating THX volume, the big sky fills with such grandiose and terrifying electricity that you feel you can't stand the wait another second. Then it gives way, and the rain comes down—recklessly, passionately, and, if you're a Texan, deliciously.

The special mood of a rainy day in Texas rarely dissipates and descends into depression; it doesn't stay around long enough. But imagine a place, a home that tapped into the relief and serenity of being inside, sheltered, on a rainy day—even as drought crazed the earth outside. Architect Max Levy has built such a house in Dallas, and he has done it without turning the house inward and without shunning the sun. He has done it, in fact, like a pioneer, employing a metal gable roof, deep overhanging eaves, a generous porch, and not one, but two dogtrots. Like his predecessors O'Neil Ford and Frank Welch, Levy doesn't sentimentalize vernacular forms but rather looks to them for the lessons they teach and the way they can be a means to achieving an honest, modernist architectural expression that is timeless.

Levy says that when he received the commission to design a house on a site overlooking a pond, he went into a kind of "elliptical orbit" imagining all the possibilities. Then he began boiling down his ideas to distill their essence into a fundamental form, in this case a long rectangular space sited on the hillside above the water. He says that if you set out to do the simple shape, you'll do something dull and banal, whereas "if you take the elliptical approach you'll *earn* the simple thing."

Along with this simple shape went a concrete floor the color of ebony and a ceiling of dark steel from Mexico, which provided a sense of shade. "That dark color is soothing," says Levy, "on a white-hot Texas day. It feels like there are rain clouds overhead." And what if it rains? Levy's answer: fifteen-inch-wide, three-inch-deep curving gutters, extending one foot below the eaves. Pure virtuosity. From the second-floor windows, dwellers can watch the rain rolling smoothly or cascading wildly into the half-moons of the metal gutters.

PREVIOUS PAGE: As in many frontier structures, one long gable (in this case, eighty feet long) spans the enclosed rooms of House above the Pond, as well as the breezeways. Deep eaves protect the house from the sun, and a generous porch opens the house to the pond, the true front of the house. Note the concrete trough that returns rainwater to the pond.

BELOW: In the core of the house, a bedroom and office on the second floor are connected across space by a bridge. The shoji screen below separates the dining room from the living and slides out beyond the frame of the house to become a design feature that Levy calls "the shoji garage."

By virtue of the gutter extensions, the eaves—already deep at four and a half feet—are more than capable of shading the house. But to foster the pleasure of shadows and retreat in a home, one must know how to manipulate light so that its life-giving aspects can bring color into a space and dance across its surfaces. For Levy, who is a faithful observer of the sun, the point is to diffuse its powers, to invite it in, he has said, "but to make it mind its manners."

The porch has often been his favored means for doing just that, and his use of it on the pond house is particularly successful. The client had a desire to view the pond from the house, but that would call for a broad western exposure, which would bring heat and glare into the house. Levy's generous screened-in porch on the western elevation became the buffer between nature and indoors, allowing the client to see the pond without squinting. By softening the light entering the house, the porch extended, by means of glass doors, its footprint.

To frame another view of the pond, he "punched" a dogtrot through his long rectangular form and opened the front door to it, as in frontier structures. He did the same at the other end of the house to create an attractive entrance for those arriving by car. There are no rocking chairs or churns, no galvanized tubs or washboards here, just the essence of the cool, shady outdoor spaces "braided" together, as he says, with a human space, by virtue of the movement across them. Rooms of the house rise up on either side of a dogtrot and the same roof hovers over all, which may be one reason Levy says that a dogtrot "takes the porch to the heart of the house."

While designing the dogtrot, a thought came to Levy: "Let's really connect the house to the pond." Having brought the theme of rain into the scheme of the house, the idea of channeling it and thus heightening the focus took hold. Water from the gutters was guided into a perpendicular gutter that bisects the breezeway and empties rainwater into vertical pipes, which pour downward into a rain pool. From there the water journeys downhill to the pond via a narrow, troughlike concrete canal.

Inside the house, living spaces rise up two stories on either side of a double-height living and dining room area, and in a recapitulation of the dogtrot idea, a metal bridge connects them across space. Another bridge through the carport dogtrot connects to an office; outside, across the entrance dogtrot, a guest suite is accessible up a steel staircase. The materials of the inside are the same as the exterior—burnished concrete blocks and finely milled fir. The clean lines and subtle colors of the materials in combination with the rice paper shoji screen create an overall Zenlike ambience.

Unlike many contemporary houses, the House above the Pond is serene—alive to its surroundings, constant in its before-the-storm calm.

BELOW: In this view toward the front door, which is entered from the dogtrot, one can see how cleanly the space is defined: A bar to the right of the frame, a staircase to the left, and even a niche for a sculpture are all cut crisply with exquisite craftsmanship out of the same wood that is also visible on the outside of the structure. The abundant use of wood was Levy's response to the client's desire to avoid gypsum board.

OPPOSITE, TOP: The dining room becomes intimate when the shoji screen is closed and the hand-painted screens to the left are lowered, hiding the kitchen and creating an elegant, enclosed space.

OPPOSITE, BELOW: The client grew up in a lavish Philip Johnson mansion; this quiet, unpretentious shelter with nature as a touchstone surely speaks to her in a different way. Here, the casual porch works as an extension of the house, modulating one's exposure to the outdoors. Screens open it to breezes and views of the pond below, and an outdoor fireplace warms it on winter days.

OVERLEAF: When visitors enter this dogtrot, they get a sweeping view not only of the pond below, but they can also see how Levy connected the house to it. Rainwater collected in the half-moon shaped gutters on the roof empties into a wide lateral gutter, then travels down through a set of pipes, which funnels it into a circular pool (seen here). It is then directed down a long concrete canal and, finally, into the pond below. This feature lures people to come listen and watch.

244

THE WOODS HOUSE

"A door to the world beyond cities"—it's a poetic thought, one that resonates particularly with architect Frank Welch, who has always, over the course of a long and illustrious career, shown his clients to such a door. His architecture has created refuge and delight in the midst of cities, but it is out beyond the fray in the hinterlands that his understanding of how to live on the land has resulted in some of Texas's most extraordinary, and often iconic, structures.

One such structure went up on the barren terrain of a vast ranch in far West Texas where the only visual boundary was the horizon line stretching endlessly in every direction. Known as the Birthday Shelter, in reference to the stacks of limestone on the site (which had been built by Mexican sheepherders as place markers and labeled "birthdays" by local ranchers), the structure possessed an archaic, monumental presence on the site. The one-room refuge was endowed only with a massive limestone fireplace and sliding doors opening broadly to the landscape. Wood from a torn-down oil derrick and cedar were the intermediate materials complementing the massive limestone structure, anchored by two pillars standing grandly and austerely against the elements. A plaque on the wall once said, "It was no will-o'-the-wisp that brought me here."

Now that structure, built in 1965 and chosen in 1997 by the Texas Society of Architects as a recipient of the 25-Year Award, has been all but destroyed by a subsequent rancher. But that shelter has an heir. Hundreds of miles away, into the landscape of far northeastern Texas, the Woods house coaxed a different idea of refuge from Welch, not one that stood up to the landscape, but rather one that slipped into it and intentionally got lost.

The Woods house sits squarely in a region known as the Cross Timbers of Texas, named for two sections of heavily forested land that cut swaths through the treeless plains of northern and central Texas. The woodland, so valued by Welch's clients, is comprised of densely growing scrub oaks. Here, the sense of interior space is twofold—the forest's interior and the home's interior—concentric spheres of insulation from the outside world.

Welch blended a forthright, clean-edged modernity with the warm, informal overtone of the house's materials and form. Beige limestone from Leuters, Texas, is comfortable in the sandy terrain of the site, and corrugated zinc—seen covering the entrance tower and defining the porch staircases—refers obliquely to the corrugation of Texas farm structures. But, in fact, Welch says the only aspect of the

MAY THIS HOUSE BE FOR OUR GENERATIONS

A DOOR TO THE WORLD BEYOND CITIES.

MAY IT REFRESH US FROM DAILY CARES.

MAY OUR FEARS RECEDE INTO ITS SHADOWS.

MAY OUR MEMORIES FORM WARMLY AT ITS HEARTH.

MAY WE KNOW GOOD MORE CLEARLY IN ITS RESPITE.

MAY PEACE BE UNTO THIS HOUSE.

—DEDICATION AT THE ENTRANCE OF THE WOODS HOUSE

PREVIOUS SPREAD: There may be no other house in this book that is more in tune with a life in nature, with living on the land. Welch understood the need for city dwellers to get away from that urban environment and into the opposite— the rustic, undeveloped countryside. He answered that need with materials appropriate to the landscape and a plan that fostered the privacy and informality desired by the client.

OPPOSITE: The patina of the soil reddens the Leuters limestone that is used in the walls. The changeable, tactile quality of this natural stone is set in relief by the sleek, industrial crispness of the zinc-coated steel tower.

house that ties it to a specific regional typology is the main entrance, which takes you from a porte cochere into a mudroom, and beyond to the kitchen.

A wide fireplace takes its place in the very center of the living room, which is itself the fundamental central link between two two-story towers—one, above the kitchen, devoted to the master suite and study; the other, rising above a game room and bedroom, accommodating two more bedrooms. Skylights in the stone-faced stairwells animate these shadow-filled spaces.

And, as if to demonstrate how vernacular form and modernity can coexist in today's world, Welch opened wide the summit of the gable roof covering the living room. Into a field of wooden strips on the ceiling, taupe-colored steel rafters rhythmically span the space, a contempory take on a lodge.

As it turns out, Welch's love of overhead light has its source in a specific, childhood moment when his parents took him to a professional photographer on the top floor of a commercial building in Sherman, Texas. The studio space was under a large skylight, and Welch was overwhelmed. It was unlike anything he had ever seen. "It was so beautiful," he says. "I became *permanently* fascinated with skylights."

Not everyone has such easy access to the very moment an idea takes hold, and there's every reason to believe that Welch's sensibility took shape in avoidance of such direct hits. He was born in Paris, Texas, on January 28, 1927. From Sherman, where he grew up, he enrolled at Texas A&M University, which in the 1940s had an architectural curriculum that fully embraced the modern movement. He studied the work of Marcel Breuer, Eero Saarinen, and Le Corbusier, and when in 1951 he received a Fulbright to study in Paris, he made a point of seeing all of Corbu's work. But he experienced it in a curious, telling way. It was a "quick vision," he says, a glimpse he was after. "I have

a funny reservation about getting too close to celebrated architects," he says. "I didn't want to fall under a spell."

Those sentiments were soon to fall under the heading of famous last words, for when Welch, back home, encountered Texas's most celebrated architect, O'Neil Ford, he immediately fell under a spell. They met in 1959 at a dinner party in a rickety garage apartment in Houston. It was a long evening. The wives and the hostesses had all fallen asleep waiting for Welch and Ford to finish talking. But the architects seemed locked in one of those rare and wonderful conversations in which a kindred spirit begins to unfold. "Ford and I talked until about three o'clock or four in the morning," Welch remembers, "and at the end he said, 'Do you want a job?'"

The job lasted only three years. Welch was eager to have his own practice and Ford encouraged him to pursue it. When the right opportunity came along, he headed to Odessa, Texas, and soon afterward next door to the oilrich culture of Midland. For the next twenty-five years he designed houses all over West Texas. In the early 1980s, he opened his current practice in Dallas.

Today, he is arguably the most respected and beloved architect in Texas. Some think of him as a direct line to Ford, but Welch refers to himself as a protégé of the man whom, he says, was a natural teacher, pointing out how things went together, the integrity of materials, the frontier sources for architectural form. But Welch was always too original to fill the role of disciple. And it is abundantly clear that Ford valued Welch's insights and opinions as only a colleague might.

In a letter of November 23, 1979, supporting Welch for fellowship in the American Institute of Architects, Ford made the point emphatically: "When asked about Frank Welch," he wrote, "one just says that he is the best architect . . . between San Antonio and Los Angeles."

BELOW: In this bedroom, the wooden ceiling is all of a piece with the side walls.

BOTTOM: In the master bedroom, Welch punched a skylight over the bed to brighten the room.

RIGHT: Welch says that the owners of this home were ideal clients—they favored cutting-edge design but were willing to accept his somewhat conservative approach because it was more directly expressive of the site on which it was built. The ceiling in the living room is split open at its apex to flood the room with natural light. Note the doors opening onto the dining room on a barndoor track, and the broad eastern porch.

OVERLEAF: The garden, with its native plants, is in keeping with the raw beauty of this north Texas landscape. The private spaces of the house, while not symmetrical, act like bookends to the gabled living room in the center. Its towering limestone chimney completes the picture of this contemporary frontier house.

ENDNOTES

Although the descriptions of the houses and the interpretations of their styles are original to me, I drew specific facts from an impressive assortment of biographies devoted to the architects. The sources listed below were particularly helpful, and I would suggest them for further reading. Where no source is mentioned, the information for the essay was gleaned from numerous interviews I conducted with architects and clients.

INTRODUCTION (pages 6–9)

The Texas Legislature adopted the State Song of Texas in 1929. William J. Marsh of Fort Worth, who composed the music, and Marsh and Gladys Yoakum, who wrote the lyrics, entered it in a statewide competition and won.

WOODLAWN (pages 12–19)

Most of my knowledge of Abner Cook and his design for Woodlawn was derived from Kenneth Hafertepe's biography, *Abner Cook: Master Builder of the Texas Frontier* (Austin: Texas State Historical Association, 1992). For references to Minard Lafever's book, see xiv; for Reverend Smoot's eulogy, pp. 189–190; early life in North Carolina and possible influences, pp. 10–11; James Shaw, p. 87. I was also aided by David Hoffman's *Woodlawn: Historic Structure Report*, prepared for the State Preservation Board, May 1999. Hoffman charts the many changes made to the house throughout its life and tells a different story than Hafertepe (which I retold) regarding Shaw's heartbreak and his decision to sell, p. 3. According to Hoffman, Shaw estimated that the house cost him $20,000.

HOUSE OF THE SEASONS (pages 20–33)

My knowledge of the House of the Seasons came as a result of interviewing the owner of the house, Richard Collins, who has done extensive research on the house. His article "A Home with a History," given to guests at the House of the Seasons, faithfully chronicles the events of Benjamin Epperson's life. The attribution of the architecture to Arthur Gilman is based on a letter to Epperson (dated 1871) from his right-hand man, J. M. Daniels. Daniels informs Epperson that Gilman would do the house for 5.5 percent of the purchase price, which he estimated would cost $12,000. Daniels recommends that he hire Gilman. Although no unequivocal evidence suggests that he did, the excellence and originality of the house augurs convincingly that he might have.

LEAGUE HOUSE (pages 34–39)

Two librarians willingly delved through their holdings, allowing me to access information on League and his relations with Nicholas Clayton. Casey Greene, head of special collections at the Rosenberg Library in Galveston, located a notation about the plans of the house in Clayton's daybook and a letter from Clayton to Mrs. League after her husband's death, asking if she could follow through on her husband's promise to make a loan of $1,000. Heather Wooten, history specialist at the Helen Hall Library in League City, provided me with helpful information on Mr. League and his wife, the former Nellie Ball. In every other respect, Barrie Scardino and Drexel Turner's monograph *The Architecture of Nicholas Clayton and His Contemporaries* (College Station: Texas

A&M University Press, 2000) was indispensable. This book provided many useful details of his life and plans of his works.

TROST HOUSE (pages 42–49)

Lloyd C. and June-Marie Engelbrechts' *Henry C. Trost: Architect of the Southwest* (El Paso: El Paso Public Library Association, 1981) is still the most exhaustive monograph on the architect to date. Their treatment of Trost's experience in Chicago and the likelihood that he worked alongside Frank Lloyd Wright in Sullivan's office are based on very suggestive evidence, of which I was convinced. Their detailed analysis of the Trost house also taught me to understand the structure in a much deeper way.

HOGG HOUSE (pages 50–57)

The excellent biography of Ayres by Robert James Coote—*The Eclectic Odyssey of Atlee B. Ayres, Architect* (College Station, Texas: A&M University Press, 2002)—furnished me with many specific details of Ayres's life: His birth, his education in New York, and, of course, his Hogg house, all found a place in my book. See especially pp. 104–107. A friend, Ed Gill of San Antonio, found a rare copy of Ayres's 1926 book, *Mexican Architecture* (New York: William Helburn, Inc.), and generously shared it with me. The depository of Ayres's drawings and letters at the Alexander Architectural Archives at the University of Texas is a gold mine of information regarding Ayres's practice. Finally, Virginia Bernhard's *Ima Hogg: The Governor's Daughter* (Austin: Texas Monthly Press, 1984) rounded out Thomas Hogg's relationship to his family, the cost of his house, his wife's efforts to find the right tile, and other pertinent details, all from primary sources.

ARMSTRONG-FERGUSON HOUSE (pages 60–67)

Very little information is available regarding Harvey Page. What I learned about him was gleaned from an obituary in the *San Antonio Express* (October 4, 1934) and from one general interest story on his work, "Harvey Page Left Architectural Legacy," in the *San Antonio Times* (May 9, 1974). He was also profiled in *Men of Affairs, a Reference Work of Prominent Men of Southwest Texas* (San Antonio Newspaper Association, 1919–20). The date of this house has been established through stylistic analysis. Architect and homeowner Ted Flato believes that its Moorish aspect predated the popularity of exotic styles in America during the 1920s. Although no hard evidence confirms it, the Craftsman aspects of the house are also suggestive of an earlier date.

KING RANCH (pages 68–79)

Information about the King Ranch or the members of the King family and their business affairs may be researched at the extensive King Ranch Archives in Kingsville, Texas, which was the source of my knowledge. Archivist Lisa Neeley provided much-needed facts regarding the house, including the iconography of the images in the Tiffany-designed stained-glass windows.

DRANE-COOK HOUSE (pages 80–89)

For the details of David Williams's life, I depended on Muriel Quest McCarthy's *David R. Williams: Pioneer Architect*, with its foreword by O'Neil Ford and introduction by Arch Swank (Dallas: Southern Methodist University Press, 1984). His time at the University of Texas is described on pp. 15–17, and his experience in Tampico is detailed on pp. 19–24; for a plan of the Drane house, see p. 71 and pp. 72–77 for archival photographs. His interest in regional architecture and the bohemian ambiance of his Dallas studio are fully treated. I also benefited from Michael Glen Wade's *David Reichard Williams: Avant-Garde Architect and Community Planner, 1890–1961* (dissertation for doctoral degree at the University of Southwestern Louisiana, July, 1978), pp. 160–69.

THE STABLE (pages 90–97)
Nearly everyone who writes about Texas architecture is indebted to Stephen Fox, who generously shares his knowledge. I am no exception. He cowrote with the late Howard Barnstone *The Architecture of John Staub*, and I went to it for the key facts regarding the design of this remarkable structure and for the circumstances under which River Oaks was developed, though space limitations forced me to greatly abbreviate their fascinating reconstruction of how it came about. For descriptions of the Stable and plans both before it was reconstructed by Staub in 1958 and afterward, see pp. 152–55. The book also provides a discerning exegesis of the taste for eclectic architecture and the work of those, like Staub, who gave it architectural voice.

CRESPI MANSION (pages 108–17)
I am indebted to Alex Fatio Taylor, daughter of Maurice Fatio, for providing me with her very interesting book, *Maurice Fatio*, a compilation of his voluminous correspondence with his family in Switzerland. Literate, conversational, and in every way engaging, the letters reveal why he was such a popular high-society architect. He describes people and projects, including the letter referenced here documenting his meeting with Crespi and his impressions of Texas. The book was privately printed. In a letter from Ms. Taylor dated May 19, 2007, she states that the house was reported to have cost $250,000. Her cousin recalled that the stone for the house was imported from Italy and that a train track (where the current North Dallas Tollway is now) allowed the stone to reach the site easily. It was stored there on the flat cars until it was used. I also learned much about the house from Robert Wiggly, Mrs. Crespi's son by a previous marriage. Archival photographs and descriptions of the Crespis occurred in a handful of newspaper articles, including "Remembrances of an Era Past," (*High Society*, Vol. 1, No. 1, March 1992, published by Society News Publications, Inc.); "The Woman's Angle," (*The Dallas Morning News*, April 19, 1954); and "The Crespi Estate," (*The Dallas Morning News*, December 30, 1984).

PARROT-ORLOWSKY HOUSE (pages 118–23)
Jann Patterson of the Meadows Museum furnished me with her excellent article "The Drawings of Charles Dilbeck," which she wrote to accompany an exhibition by the same name at the Meadows Museum. The scope of her research went beyond a discussion of his drawings, to the facts of his early life, his move to Dallas, his prolific work for developers there, and an informative analysis of his style. Dilbeck's widow, Pat Dilbeck, was also an excellent source of information regarding his character. And architectural historian Willis Winters, who is writing a biography of Dilbeck, was an informative sounding board and a great resource, providing me with the specific date for the house I had chosen and the name of the original client. *Dallas Morning News* architecture critic David Dillon contrasted Dilbeck's interest in the frontier houses of the Panhandle and West Texas with Ford and Williams's fascination with the homes of Germans and Poles in central Texas in "Dilbeck, Meyer and Ford" (*Dallas Life Magazine*, October 6, 1985).

BROMBERG HOUSE (pages 126–33)
Mary Carolyn Hollers George's *O'Neil Ford, Architect* (College Station: Texas A&M Press, 1992), covers the scope of the architect's long and illustrious career. I benefited particularly from her interview with Juanita Bromberg on July 12, 1984. Her notes not only included Williams's comment that Ford was a better architect than he because he had not attended architecture school, but they also quote Mrs.

Bromberg about the fees Ford requested, as well as the fact that Lynn Ford copied the gadroon pattern in the links of a favorite bracelet she owned. A conversation with Alan Bromberg personalized the project by recalling his impressions as a child of Ford and Arch Swank on the job. Touring the house with Frank Welch was perhaps the most revealing, as he pointed out the qualities of Ford's work that still filled him with awe.

NAGEL HOUSE (pages 134–41)
The Alexander Architectural Archives at the University of Texas at Austin has among its holdings Nagel's papers and plans of his architectural projects. I was able to read the avid correspondence he had with Gropius during his brief hiatus from Cambridge in the early 1940s and during World War II. The current owner of the house, David Rabban, generously loaned me all of the documents that had been handed down to him from the previous owner, which included the application forms to qualify it for the National Register of Historic Places and Austin architect Tom Shefelman's profile of Chester Nagel, which contributed greatly to my essay.

DE MENIL HOUSE (pages 142–51)
In the early 1980s I had the opportunity to visit the house while Mrs. de Menil still lived there. Although she was not there at the time of my visit, the impression of her and the life she lived was palpable. Artworks were everywhere, filling every surface in such a rich abundance of styles and periods that the house seemed to be little more than a backdrop for the art. Now, of course, it is possible to appreciate it as a work of architecture and to see in its greatness the flexibility of this International Style home. Details about Johnson's experience with the de Menils were drawn from Frank Welch's *Philip Johnson & Texas* (Austin: The University of Texas Press, 2000, pp. 38-51). For a plan, see p. 50.

LIPSHY HOUSE (pages 152–59)
Regrettably, no monograph exists at the present time chronicling the life and career of Howard Meyer. However, *Dallas Morning News* architecture critic David Dillon interviewed Meyer before his death in 1984 and wrote an informative profile of him as part of his coverage of the 1981 renovation of the Lipshy house by Mr. and Mrs. James Clark Jr. Dillon's feature story, "The Second Time Around," appeared on February 5, 1983. All the details of Meyer's early career, as well as my knowledge of what had befallen the Lipshy house before the Clarks bought it, were drawn from his piece.

DURST-GEE HOUSE (pages 160–71)
Although Larry Grantham, the Goff apprentice and primary builder of the house, died in 2002, I was able to contact his friend and fellow builder Jim Veal, who practices architecture in Pensacola, Florida. Veal explained the reference of the plan to the circular form of the cul-de-sac.

BASS HOUSE (pages 178–87)
See "Texas Tour de Force" by Mildred F. Schmertz (*House & Garden*, Vol. 163, No. 12, December 1991, pp. 164–73). See also Mark Gunderson's "Rudolph and Texas," (*Texas Architect*, May/June 1998, pp. 50–52) and "Enigmas of Architecture" by Paul Rudolph (*Architecture and Urbanism*, 1977, pp. 317–20). The quote I used came from page 320 of this journal.

STRETTO HOUSE (pages 190–99)
Steven Holl, "From Concept to Realization," *Stretto House* (New York: Monacelli Press, 1996), pp. 6–9. See also Kenneth Frampton's monograph *Steven Holl, Architect* (New York: Phaidon Press, 2007).

KNIGHTS' GAMBIT (pages 200–211)
Epigraph from Ottilie Fuchs Goeth's *Memoirs of a Texas Pioneer Grandmother*, with translation, research, and additions by Irma Goeth Guenther (Burnet, Texas: Eakin Press, 1982), p. 43.

SOURCES

WOODLAWN
ARCHITECT: Tom Hatch of hatch + ulland owen architects, Austin
INTERIOR DESIGN: Mary Ames and Mark Ashby
CONTRACTOR: Richard Gift
LANDSCAPE DESIGN: Lambert's, Dallas

HOUSE OF THE SEASONS
RESTORATION ARCHITECT: Wayne Bell, FAIA of Bell, Klein & Hoffman
INTERIOR RESTORATION: the late Dr. Anna Brighton of the University
   of Texas, Austin

TROST HOUSE
The interiors designed by Henry Trost in 1909 are intact and
maintained by Robert McGregor, whose family purchased the home
and its furnishings in 1958 from an owner who had kept the house as
Trost had left it.

ARMSTRONG-FERGUSON HOUSE
INTERIOR DESIGN: Gwen Griffith of San Antonio and Fern Santini of
   Abode, Inc., Austin
LANDSCAPE DESIGN: Sarah Lake Landscape Design and Rosa Finsley
   of Kings Creek Landscaping

HALBREICH HOUSE
INTERIOR DESIGN: the late Marguerite Green; her former partner, Paul
   Garzotto; Emily Summers of Emily Summers Design Associates;
   and John Bobbitt
GARDEN DESIGN: Paul N. Fields, ASLA, President of Lambert's and
   Larry C. Speed, Senior Garden Manager
TILE PAINTER OF THE ORANGERIE: Cathy Schermer

BROMBERG HOUSE
RESTORATION ARCHITECT: Frank Welch of Frank Welch & Associates
INTERIOR DESIGNER: Josie McCarthy of Josie McCarthy Associates
LANDSCAPE ARCHITECT: David Rolston of David Rolston Landscape
   Architects

DE MENIL HOUSE
RESTORATION ARCHITECT: Stern and Bucek Architects
RESTORATION OF CHARLES JAMES'S FABRICS: Hilary Crady
LANDSCAPE RESTORATION: Jane Anderson Curtis

LIPSHY HOUSE
INTERIOR DESIGN AND ARCHITECTURAL RESTORATION: Bodron + Fruit
LANDSCAPE ARCHITECT: Jeff Bargas

WILSON HOUSE
INTERIOR DESIGN: Pat Wood of Waldrop's, Abilene
LANDSCAPE DESIGN: Naud Burnett Associates

BASS HOUSE
LANDSCAPE DESIGN: Robert Zion, green landscape, and Russell Page,
   garden design

STRETTO HOUSE
LANDSCAPE DESIGN: Rosa Finsley of Kings Creek Landscaping

KNIGHTS' GAMBIT
INTERIOR DESIGN: Watkins Baker Design, Trina Stanfield Design
METALWORK: Eric Stevenson

LASATER HOUSE
LANDSCAPE DESIGN: Rosa Finsley of Kings Creek Landscaping

NOWLIN HOUSE
ARCHITECT: Paul Lamb with Ted Young, Philip Kyle, Pam Chandler
INTERIOR DESIGN: Fern Santini of Abode, Inc., Austin
LANDSCAPE DESIGN: Richard Fadal of TexaScapes
CONTRACTOR: David Escobedo of Escobedo Construction
IRONWORK: Joseph Pehoski, Pehoski Metal Smiths in Salado
STONE CARVING: Bob Ragan of Texas Carved Stone
EXTERIOR FRIEZES, BALL COURT RINGS, ETC.: Philippe Kleinfelter
GILDED PLASTER FRIEZE IN DINING ROOM AND ELSEWHERE: Rick Eddy
BUFFET IN DINING ROOM AND OTHER FURNITURE: Jean Paul Viollet
GLASS LIGHT FIXTURES IN LOGGIA: Kathleen Ash

HOUSE ABOVE THE POND
INTERIOR DESIGN: Paul Draper and Associates
LANDSCAPE ARCHITECT: Mesa Design
CONTRACTOR: Don Romer

WOODS HOUSE
INTERIOR DESIGN: Punkin Peterson Power
GARDEN DESIGN: Debra Fox

ACKNOWLEDGMENTS

There are clearly many more than twenty-five great houses in Texas, and I am painfully aware of those left off this stage. The extraordinary imaginations of James Riley Gordon and Alfred Giles come to mind, as do the fine homes of Houston's Birdsall Briscoe and, in a more modern vein, those by Dallas's Bud Oglesby. Frank Lloyd Wright designed homes for the state, as did my particular pal, the virtuoso Harwell Hamilton Harris, but they too were passed over. What I hope to say is that Texas has fostered the talents of many excellent architects—it is perhaps more true now than ever before, but I forced myself to pick and choose my way through to those few houses that were not only great in and of themselves, but also enabled me to tell a story about Texas design in words and in telling pictures by the masterful Grant Mudford.

I am grateful to the many people who allowed me into the sacred domains of their homes and especially those who endured the sometimes long days of photo shoots. Many of the owners provided lunch for us—homemade *carne guisada* at King Ranch stands out, as does a celebratory dinner in Houston, compliments of Clint Jeu, who met us at Goff's Gee house in his sister Julia Gee's absence. (After learning that it was my birthday, he pre-arranged an open line of credit at a wonderful Italian restaurant for us and my family, who had joined me.)

Others took me in simply to give me rest and a chance to recoup. Among those, I'd especially like to thank my good friend Janie McGarr in Dallas, whose door was always open to me, and my cousin Jean "T. J." Beck, who took me in after several long days in Houston. They were supportive and interested, and in debriefing them, I often found the very words that ended up in the text of this book. When Grant and his assistant Darrin Little arrived and we began to travel the state, I was grateful for the hospitality of my cousin Cary Meeks and his wife, Marissa; Tom and Nettie Wilson, the owners of the Wilson house; and Richard Collins and Shirley Reiman of the House of the Seasons. And throughout it all, I was thankful for Becky Jackson who, since our meeting at age three, has been a rock of support and a refuge for virtually my entire life.

Texas scholars and architects will handily guess whose consultation I sought early on: Houston's Stephen Fox, whose knowledge of Texas residential architecture is legendary, as is his generosity. Fort Worth architect Mark Gunderson opened many doors for me and enthusiastically shared his own extensive knowledge of the state's architecture. Texas scholar Jerry Buttrey loaned me books with fascinating accounts of early Texas life, and, as far as that goes, I was always grateful for T. R. Fehrenbach's page-turning *Lone Star*, continually testifying that fiction, when it comes to Texas history, has nothing on fact.

I am grateful to Richard Olsen who, representing Harry N. Abrams, Inc., encouraged me to write a proposal for a book on great Texas homes and, afterward, faithfully shepherded it through the decision process. From the beginning, I appreciated Abrams' editor in chief Eric Himmel for his friendliness toward the project and me. I am grateful for the sensitivity of designer Darilyn Carnes, who cast my words and Grant's photos into such an elegant and inviting final product. I was always happy to hear Laura Tam's voice on my phone when she called to check on details of the book or to answer my frequent questions. But it is to my editor, Andrea Danese, that I owe the most heartfelt thanks. Somehow, with her special brand of wisdom and forbearance, she lifted me out of the quagmires that dogged my springtime of writing and pulled the prose from my pen (as it were), meeting each new installment with genuine interest and excitement. Although I have never met her in person, she has entered, as Yeats would have it, "the deep heart's core" of friendship.

And then there is Grant Mudford, my collaborator. No one believed that he would accept the job, that he would actually take a month out of his schedule, turning down dozens of more lucrative offers, to drive around Texas shooting houses. But he did. I think there was something about his experience growing up in Australia with a father who loved Jimmie Rodgers that imbued Grant with a distinct interest in (and real affection for) Texas. He brought some of those Jimmie Rodgers CDs with him, and, as "the father of country music" yodeled out the blues in the background, we traveled down Texas highways for miles and miles—a very merry threesome. Grant and Darrin had first met up with me in El Paso at the end of October 2006, pulling in from Los Angeles with a new van absolutely laden with photography equipment, as well as other key supplies—almonds, sodas, Trader Joe's coffee, the Motel 6 guidebook, and sake—that seem now like the symbols of our sojourn. Night after night, after long days of driving or shooting, we'd check into the local Motel 6, I'd get a call to come over and cap the day off with a glass of sake, and then we'd hunt (at the lovable Darrin's behest) for the nearest roadside steak house. We never talked about the houses in the evening, but daily, as I watched Grant frame the shots, Darrin move equipment (loading and fastidiously unloading film), and as I stared deeply into the Polaroids, I knew that the book would be beautiful and that I would always be grateful that Grant had said "yes."

Finally, I want to thank my family, who heroically bore the brunt of the project. My twin seven-year-old sons, Phineas and Atticus, who too often witnessed their mother wringing her hands or frantically pounding the keyboard, were always good-natured about the project. The children of a conceptual artist, they were genuinely sorry to tell me that the tools of my trade weren't as enticing as those of their father's. And it is to this father, Mel Ziegler, that I owe the deepest gratitude. Although he is not a Texan, he saw the landscape with fresh eyes and helped me appreciate many of the lovely aspects I had taken for granted. He was the first to believe that I was right for the project, he shouldered the demands of two small children (in very imaginative ways), and he sweetly listened to the words of my stories in the wee, small hours of the morning, offering sound advice and support.

In an unexpected twist of fate, which occurred after I had started working on this book in earnest, the boys and I followed Mel to Tennessee, where he had accepted a post at Vanderbilt University. I am strangely aware that I have returned to the state my ancestors left more than a hundred years ago, bound for the land on the far side of the Red River. I'm in Nashville—"Music City." It's a lovely place and an adventure, but you should know that as I write these final words, I am, as my new neighbor and fellow expatriate Nanci Griffith has put it, "in a Lone Star state of mind."

Editor: Andrea Danese
Designer: Darilyn Lowe Carnes
Production Manager: Alison Gervais

Library of Congress Cataloging-in-Publication Data

Germany, Lisa.
  Great houses of Texas / Lisa Germany ; photography by Grant Mudford.
    p. cm.
  ISBN 978-0-8109-9393-8
  1. Architecture, Domestic—Texas. 2. Architecture and society—Texas. I. Mudford, Grant, 1944- II. Title.

  NA7235.T4G47 2008
  728.09764—dc22

                    2007041800

Printed and bound in China
10 9 8 7 6 5 4 3 2 1

HNA ■▯■■■
harry n. abrams, inc.
a subsidiary of La Martinière Groupe
115 West 18th Street
New York, NY 10011
www.hnabooks.com